From the best-selling author of
Fire Up! MLM Nuts $ Bolts, The Master Pres
The Lady of the Rings, Let's Party,
Co-Author of *Go Diamond* and *True Le*

MW00905208

A Powerful Network Marketing Phone Guide

JAN RUHE

www.janruhe.com

Make That Call

Copyright © 2005 by Jan Ruhe

All rights reserved. Reproduction or translation of any part of this work beyond that permitted by Section 107 or 108 of the 1976 United States Copyright Act without the permission of the copyright owner is unlawful. Requests for permission or further information should be addressed to the author. Every effort has been made to locate the copyright owner of material in this book. Omission brought to our attention will be corrected in subsequent editions. This book contains Jan Ruhe's opinions and personal experiences. Her opinions do not necessarily reflect those of her company, or any persons living or dead unless directly stated.

ISBN 0-9702667-7-4
LCCN: 2005901680

Jan Ruhe
www.janruhe.com

Cover Design and Graphic Art
by Sarah Rose McKinley.

Published by Proteus Press
300 Puppy Smith, Suite 205-290, Aspen, CO 81611
tel. 970-927-9380
fax 970-927-0112

Dedication

*To my precious children, Sarah, Clayton and Ashley,
to my soul mate, partner and husband Bill
and to all of my students worldwide.*

*Also-
Bilbo Baggens of Glenwood Shire
January 21, 2002 - December 8, 2004*

*During the productions of our last three books
and while working with our graphic artist, David,
Bilbo was always there, happy and energetic.
He will be missed!*

****

There Comes A Day

*"There is a day you get into Network Marketing, but nothing
happens until the day that Network Marketing gets into you."*
-Jan Ruhe

Grow A Shade Tree

*"The noblest thing a person can do is
to plant a tiny seed that someday will
grow into an incredible tree that will
give shade to those they will never know."*
-Jan Ruhe

A Message From Jan Ruhe

Twenty-five years ago someone made a phone call that changed my life for the better forever. One call, one invitation...what a difference one phone call made. Zoom forward 25 plus years. Because of that **one** phone call, today I am a millionaire, have raised three fabulous children, and live the lifestyle only a few can experience. Thank God someone made that one phone call to simply invite me to a home party. That is when fate took a turn and my life journey began. I cannot even imagine how my life would have turned out if someone had not made that one call.

Build your Network Marketing business for yourself and those you love. In my career, I believe I have made more than 100,000 phone calls myself. So can you. Just believe you can, increase your communication skills and get started. It's so important that you don't put off your future any longer.

> Grab your phone and get to work.
> Go for being the top distributor in your company.
> Take urgent, massive action!

Get Focused

The more people you talk to, the faster your Network will grow. It's my hope that *Make That Call* will be the catalyst you need to take the activity that will promote you. Get focused on making calls and use the ideas in this book to build and create the most incredible future so that you can have residual income forever.

Uncertainty To Certainty

The biggest challenge I have seen in Network Marketing, virtually everywhere I go, is the tremendous amount of uncertainty most distributors have about *if* they can succeed. You too may be facing a fair share of uncertainty in your belief right now as well. That's the reason I wrote this book, to give you *more confidence* and *courage* to make more calls.

Take New Actions

Taking new actions is the only way to produce new results. I want to help you dramatically increase the quality of your life. This book includes specific how-to's, stories, examples and scripts for you to experience. You want to enjoy the lifestyle while you still have time to enjoy, benefit and profit from it. You want to live with abundance and prosperity, sail through your fears and troubles, and soar to the stars; take a leap of faith, have a band of hope, and learn ideas to apply immediately to get massive improvement. Push and stretch yourself for constant long-term pleasure and enduring enjoyment of life. You are extremely powerful. Get a clear vision of where your life can be in the future.

Fall In Love With Calling

You gotta love what's cooking, you can't heat an oven with snowballs, if you don't love what you are doing and can't stay fired up to get the job done, you might as well not even read this book. Never stop looking for ideas to speed up the process of succeeding.

J.O.B.=
JUST OUTSTANDING BENEFITS

Success-Certain Strategies

Confront your fears with *"Success-certain"* strategies, skills, scripts and words. This will enable you to break through your fears in a matter of seconds, instead of being held back by them for years. Your personal potential is unlimited. I think you also suspect this to be true, but you may not know how to precisely tap into your own unlimited potential. You might get empowered for a few days, but that's not enough. Get fired up for life! Start your path to the top today!

I Made The Calls Because I Wanted The Lifestyle

Those who make the calls are going to learn some lessons that are very difficult to teach. Lessons can be taught in Network Marketing that are difficult to get across in the home, church or classroom. They are lessons of discipline, sacrifice and teamwork. Watching a distributor apply these lessons and succeed in their career is a big part of my pleasure as a trainer in the industry worldwide.

Make Today The Day

Start today to make that call! Truly *want* to get started today. What are you waiting for? Why not make today *the* day that you decide to go for greatness and show the world what you can accomplish? There truly is no view like the view from the top. Your fabulous future starts today.

Come To The Table Of Plenty

One phone call might change the direction of your life forever for the better. How many calls would you make to find that one person who will take you to the top? You *can* have the lifestyle. If it's attainable for one, it's attainable for all. Here is to your colossal success! Come to the table of plenty, there is a place waiting for you. Making the calls is the price tag that you have to make to leap over mediocrity. It's your turn to shine. I wish you wealth, health and happiness. As I say to you now and always, *don't be average, be a champion.*

Jan Ruhe

> *"Jan Ruhe has motivated distributors to do more than they thought possible including us. Spending time with her, you can tell she was willing to make more calls than anyone we know. We have been her students, and friends for years. Read this book and take action. You will be so glad you did."*
> -Steve and Debbie Roper

TABLE OF CONTENTS

CHAPTER ONE
THE BIG PICTURE

The big picture of growing a Network Marketing business is simple. The distributor is the advertiser for products that are bought in huge quantities by a corporation and are moved through independent distributors in to the hands of the masses. Those who move the most products out of the warehouse get paid the most. It all comes down to talking to more people. Here is the big picture:

1. **Recruit thousands of distributors and teach them to do a little bit, often.**
2. **Build leaders and make THEM successful.**

It's Up To Me

Sarah, my daughter, was 4 years old, and my son Clayton was 2 years old. I was a stay at home mother and not happy with our financial situation. I wanted more for my children. We always had too much month at the end of the money. I realized that if I was going to be able to give my children what I wanted to give them, that I needed to make some extra money from home. It was all up to me. My mantra became, *"If it's going to be, it's up to me!*

One call can change a future of not just one life but of thousands of new distributors and millions of people getting a product that makes a difference.

A Call That Changed My Life

In 1979, *I received a phone call,* and lucky for me I answered my phone, for in those days there were no answering machines. The caller invited me to a home party. The caller said she was having a few mothers of my daughter Sarah's classmates over to her home. Sarah was attending the prestigious, private Lamplighter School in Dallas, Texas, and her early education was extremely important to me. The caller told me that the products that would be shown were educational toys, books, puzzles and tabletop games. Boom! I was interested in attending big time! It wasn't until March, 1980 that I joined my company. My entire story is in my book: *MLM Nuts $ Bolts.* Available at www.janruhe.com.

Work With Your Hostess

Not only was I interested in the products but I was looking for something to do from home to make some extra money. The reason I was so excited to go was that the hostess thought I might be interested in seeing these products. Her child was a playmate of Sarah's, and if she was interested in the products for her child, then I wanted to know about them, too. I was mesmerized, excited and interested when I walked in the door. The distributor had not made the call.

Hint: The hostess had made the call. I was intrigued and excited before the distributor opened her mouth! I wanted to join on the spot! Get your hostess excited about having a party and your products!

If at first you do succeed, try something harder.

The Promise

In the early years of Network Marketing, you do a lot and get paid very little. In your later years in Network Marketing, you get paid a lot for doing very little.

Three Infallible Rules For Powerful Results

Rule #1: Talk to more people.

Rule #2: Talk to more people.

Rule #3: Talk to more people.

S.T.P.

See The People

Sell The People

Share The Plan

Share The Possibilities

Seek The People

Seek The Passion

God gives every bird it's food, but he does not throw it into it's nest.

There Has To Be A Better Way

Script to chitchat with friends:

"Getting an 8-5 job was not an option. I hated having a boss, power struggles, seeing the same people every day, having a glass ceiling, and men having the better paying jobs. I was not interested in falling into the trap of needing company benefit packages, or having to ask off for vacations. That life was not for me. Putting my children in daycare was absolutely not an option. They were my life. I was not going to let someone else enjoy their growing up years, no matter how great that person might be. I was not going to miss my children's childhood. I went hunting for something to do to change the direction I was going. I thought about you and what you are going through and know, without a doubt, that this business could be for you too!"

Make your own script here:

_____

_____

_____

_____

_____

_____

_____

_____

Increased Opportunity

When you use the telephone, your chances of getting a prospect to take some action are hundreds of times better than through the mail. You can answer questions, find out what the prospect is thinking about, and build your business faster.

Which One Are You?

It takes the same amount of energy to go from average to successful, as it takes to go from average to mediocre. The type of activity is what makes the difference.

The Extremely Successful

Volume Increasing = Makes Things Happen

Those Who Remain Average

Volume Sustaining = Watch What Happens

Those Who Stay Mediocre

Volume Decreasing = Wonders "What Happened?"

> *If you are in a rowboat on a big lake, and a bad storm comes up, pray, but row for the shore.*

Phone Ease

Today you can keep in touch along your daily path. You can easily make phone calls from everywhere. Staying in touch is paramount. Daily communication, voice mail, conference calls, personal calls and training calls are all part of growing a Network Marketing business.

The Six C's Of Phone Skills

1. Clarity in information for the call.
2. Commitment to make the call.
3. Consistency of making the call.
4. Confidence to make the call.
5. Controlling your time to make the call.
6. Call to action of those listening.

Use The Phone Wisely

Those who embrace the phone and *use it wisely* can have an amazing future. The operating words are to use it wisely. If you just want to gossip, talk to side-lines and others who have no vested interest in your success, you are wasting lifetime. Period. Stop all nonsense phone calls that get you upset, worried and that have absolutely no value.

A Promising Future

Prospect: *"You seem so excited about what you are doing, tell me more…"*

Distributor: *"I heard when I joined Network Marketing about residual income but at first, I did not understand what they were talking about. But once I understood I got so fired up and now **I have got to tell you about it!** You must listen to me! What I have gotten involved in is in integrity and it is achievable for both of us to have an incredible future. You <u>must</u> listen to what I have to say. It's urgent that I speak to you."*

Associate With Successful Distributors

You can increase your enthusiasm and in some measure increase your success if you make a habit of associating with distributors who have become successful. When you seek out successful distributors, listen to what they say. Ask for their opinions and advice. You will find that almost all successful distributors will help you. It is important to keep your association with successful distributors a two-way street. Be willing to share your ideas too.

How To Make Money

Prospect: *"So, how do you make money in this business?"*

Distributor: *"The more products you move out of the company warehouse, the more you earn."*

Developing Great New Skills

To be a success in Network Marketing, simply talk to more people about joining the opportunity. The more you talk about your opportunity, the more prospects you will have. The more skills you develop to communicate your opportunity, the more quality prospects you will get. Success happens for those distributors who consistently get what they want by providing valuable service to others. They set and achieve goals that benefit others as well as themselves. Bottom line, they simply talk to more people.

Learn Communication Skills

New Distributor: *"How do you suggest that I get started?"*

Distributor: *"Duplicate everything you can to learn how to communicate with more people. Work on your presentation skills, have a Rhino Spirit, and press onward and upward towards the top of the Compensation Plan. I am going to show you the way and will not let you fail. The only way you can fail is to quit."*

> It's always too soon to quit.

Be A Sponge

Take in any and all information. Choose later what you want to keep and what you need to discard. Take the best and leave the rest.

Get A Powerful Philosophy

Make up your own or borrow mine. *"Lead me and show me how to do it, follow me once I figure it out, and if you aren't interested in going for greatness, get out of my way."*

Network Marketing Explained

Prospect: *"I hear that only those at the top or only a few make any money at that business."*

Distributor: *"The distributors who make the most money are those who move the most products out of the company warehouse. There are two ways to do this: 1. Move product by yourself or 2. Sponsor others to do the same. You don't have to struggle to succeed. Just focus on moving product and you will have a thriving, pulsating business."*

Know Your Specific Message

You can blast your message from the tallest billboards; flash it on the big screen; broadcast it over the airwaves and paste it across the daily news. But where will it get you? If it's not the right message to the right target audience, it will never get you in the position you really want.

Someone Is Joining Now

Somewhere, right now, someone is quitting Network Marketing and giving up. At the same time, someone is joining and has ignited their passion to succeed.

Learn Product Knowledge

It's important to develop sound product knowledge. You want to become an expert. A basic knowledge of what the benefits of your products are, supported by a number of illustrations (which you can learn from books, seminars, videos, other people's testimonials, as well as your own experiences), will provide information to make successful calls and excite new prospects to join you.

The degree to which you are willing to put yourself into personal growth and leadership development will determine the success you achieve in Network Marketing.

Personal Growth And Development

Distributor to budding leaders: *"I am committed to you, to your success and to your leadership development. You need to know that I am not committed to your comfort. When you decide you truly want to succeed and go to the top, you will need to put yourself into self-development. There will be things you will be doing that may be uncomfortable for you. Beginning a Network Marketing business is no different from starting any other business. There will be growing pains, and I am committed to supporting you through those times. So, do I have your permission to speak to you as a leader out of my commitment to your success?"*

Attend Regular Trainings

The more you learn, the more you earn. When you attend meetings, listen for the one idea or one piece of information that can motivate you to get on the phone. Attend business briefings, conferences, conventions and meetings around kitchen tables. Don't have analysis paralysis and have to analyze everything before you get started. Earn while you learn.

Read Books On Network Marketing

Readers are leaders and leaders are readers. The more you study Network Marketing the more you will find amazing ideas in books written by those who have walked before you. Information shared in these books will help you succeed quicker than reinventing the wheel. There are great books, audios and DVD's available at www.janruhe.com.

Listen To CD's

Turn your car into a rolling classroom. Make sure you pop a CD in your car and begin to listen to powerful ideas, philosophies, how–to, and enthusiasm. As you listen, you will find information that will give you more confidence to get on the phone more to build your business.

Make A Binder

As you are collecting ideas, write them in your logs (see pages, 117, 118, 119) so that you don't forget important information that you learn. Practice new ideas by getting on the phone, find what works. Keep the best; toss the rest.

The Law Of Averages

The law of averages works this way: the more you do the more you achieve. So, the more calls you make, the more interviews or appointments you obtain; the larger the number of planned interviews, the greater the number of presentations; the more opportunities you get to close sales and get recruits. The higher the number of recruits and sales, the larger your volume of sales and income will be. You can make more calls with no additional time expenditure by planning your day, your time, and who you call.

If you continue to do the same thing the same way over and over again, under the same circumstances, it will produce a set of results that will always stay the same. Here is a typical average in Network Marketing *Law of Averages*. Out of every 10 people you talk to, who LISTEN to your presentation, 6 get excited about it and say they will join you. However, only 3 actually join and get started and one of those 3 really works the business. So every 10 times you share your plan, you should end up with one possible productive long-term distributor. To improve your averages, don't just call anybody. You want to get referrals and find potential good prospects to call. Then, make the call.

The Gateway To Your Future

Think about what your phone calls are ultimately going to bring to your business achievement. Set your mind to consider the enjoyable parts of getting on the phone. Spend concentrated times making your calls. Enjoy making calls. The phone is the gateway to your fabulous future.

Important Questions For The Distributor

Put the answers to these questions to work and increase your sales and income:

* How can I raise the dollar value of my selling time?
* How can I raise the number of appointments I obtain per call made?
* How can I raise the number of calls I make each week?
* How can I raise the number of new prospects I see each week?
* How can I raise the number of presentations I give per appointment?
* How can I raise the number of recruits I get per call?
* How can I raise the number of repeat sales I succeed in making on the calls?

> *"There are simply no limits to what you can accomplish."*
> -Jayne Leach

Get A Strong Identity

We are in sales. We are in the convincing, persuading and sorting business. We sort through the public to find more distributors.

Prospect: *"What do you do?"*

Distributor: *"I am in sales. I am the top recruiter in my company. I have the most incredible job on the planet. I am the advertising arm for my company and I am so excited about what I do. I would love to let you know about it so that you can decide whether or not it's for you!"*

Time Cannot Be Replaced

You can always get more money, but you can't get more time. What you do today will pay off in the upcoming years. Be the one who says, *"I am so glad I got into Network Marketing and worked the plan."* Instead of those who say, *"I had a chance to do something with my life and squandered my lifetime, I wish I had made Network Marketing work."* Get a sense of urgency; time is ticking by…tick tock…tick tock.

The Best Time To Call

Seventy-five percent of all calls are not completed on the first attempt. Increase your chances of completing your calls by calling in the mornings and evenings from Tuesday to Friday. The worst time to make calls is on Monday morning or late night. These times should be avoided unless the call is absolutely necessary. There are exceptions to the rules. Many prospects' availability often is directly linked to their occupation.

Timing Of Calls Is Important

There are two important times during the day for you to make the call.

1. Immediately after you have completed a successful phone call and
2. Immediately after you have failed to have a successful phone call.

You want to get back on the phone after being rejected and keep calling. When you have success, you want to get back on the phone and build upon that success.

Ask yourself: *"Why am I going to make this call?"*

Wasting Time On The Phone

Small talk is a huge squanderer of time. Only talk on the phone for social reasons after you reach your goals.

Managing Phone Time Wisely

Here are specific ways to make use of the time you have to make the calls:

* Organize most of your calls so that they can be made all at the same time.
* Plan your calls for times that increase your chances of reaching the prospect.

> *Productivity is directly connected to how you utilize your time.*

Conserve Phone Time

* When you call a prospect, inquire about the timing of your call to see if you have interrupted something important. You have no way of knowing what the prospect's doing. It may be a bad time to call. This might stop you from achieving your objective. Ask, *"Is this a good time for you to talk."* This approach also shows you care about the prospect.
* Once your business is done on the phone, try to bring the call to an end before the prospect does.

> *"Advice to the foolish is like rain on barren ground."*
> -Medhi

Ask yourself: *"If this one call is successful, what will the result be?"* You will never know if you don't make that call.

Explore The Possibilities

Explore the possibilities, master your emotions and take any path you choose. You can be as successful as you desire. Time is not waiting and will not wait for you, it is up to you to get started. The big questions for you to answer are why not you and why not now? If not you, then who? Who will achieve and succeed? Why continue to watch others succeed when it could certainly be you?

Busy Bodies

There are distributors who are gossips and talk way too much to anyone who will listen to them. They have the scoop on everyone. If they can get you to think that you are close friends, and you open up even a small bit to them, they will then pass your private business on to someone else. This is a HUGE, massive waste of lifetime. The busy bodies will keep calling until they will find someone who they can waste time with. Spend your time making calls that get results.

Drain People

There are people who will try to keep you on the phone and who are unproductive. Be clear from the beginning of a call with someone like this that you only have a certain amount of time you can give them per call.

Need A Phone Buddy?

There are distributors who have to have a buddy. They want to talk to other distributors not about building the business, but all kinds of subjects. Spend your time making calls that get results.

If It's Not One Thing, It's Your Mother

Many times, parents want to talk to their grown children on a daily basis. When you **work** from home, some parents don't understand that you do work from home. They think you have plenty of time to hang on the phone with them. Quantity of time is not as important as the quality of time spent. Make sure your parents understand that you can talk to them early in the morning or late at night, because during the day you are working on building your business.

M. I. N.

Ask yourself during the day, is what I am doing the **m**ost **i**mportant thing I should be doing right **n**ow? If not, should I be on the phone? If your lips are moving, you should be pointing or dialing. Be pointing to a PowerPoint slide show, pointing to circles on a napkin, sharing the Compensation Plan or on the phone searching for new distributors.

Most Important Now

Make Calls That Get Results

There are distributors who call each other at least 20 times per day. They know everything there is to know about each other's private and personal life and they know about each other's business. They both are delightful distributors but have wasted a great deal of business building time being in such close contact. If they had spent that same time contacting prospects, and making productive calls, they could have had a much bigger business.

How To Get Off The Phone

Distributor: *"I have enjoyed talking with you, and I know you are busy also. I will send you the information you requested tomorrow."*

Believe in What You Do

Network Marketing is a plan that is solid. It works for everyone who has goals, dreams, visions, wants, needs and desires. I never asked how much money I would make when I first got involved. It just looked like something I would enjoy doing and I wanted to join. I had no idea the company was brand new. I didn't care about anything else but creating a fabulous lifestyle for my children. Most people don't do well in Network Marketing unless they really believe in what they are selling and that the opportunity to earn income is real.

Setting The Record Straight

When building a Network Marketing business on the phone there are no magic tricks, no shortcuts, no *"easy"* ways, no get-there-fast gimmicks that always work. It just doesn't happen. The fundamental task of marketing has nothing to do with getting the message inside anyone's head. The goal of marketing is to instead understand what's going on inside the customer's head so well that you are able to create a message that harmonizes with what the prospect is thinking. It is not what we want to sell that counts, but what the prospect values that must occupy our attention.

Make calls every day in a serious way!

Don't Stew....Do

Once you decide to go for it, burn all bridges behind you, giving yourself no way to retreat!

The Top Four Ways To Increase Production

There are only four ways in which you can achieve an increase in your total volume of sales. Unless you manage to tap one of these sources, whatever effort you make or whatever plan of work you may set up is doomed to failure.

1. Calling on a greater number of high potential prospects. Make nine calls a day instead of eight. Plan your time better and devote more of your time to actually making calls.
2. Close a greater percentage of prospects you call. Work on closing three prospects out of eight instead of two out of eight.
3. Selling larger quantities per order. Instead of selling one product, go for ten.
4. Have a wide range of products. Sell your full line, rather than only the *"easy-sell"* items. Acquire a thorough knowledge of your products.

"Work from eight to faint."
-Jeff Roberti

It's not what you know, it's what you show!

I Will Persist Until I Succeed

"I will persist until I succeed. I was not delivered unto this world in defeat, nor does failure course in my veins. I am not a sheep waiting to be prodded by my shepherd. I am a lion and I refuse to talk, to walk or to sleep with the sheep. The slaughterhouse of failure is not my destiny. The prizes of life are at the end of each journey, not near the beginning; and it is not given to me to know how many steps are necessary in order to reach my goal. Failure I may still encounter at the thousandth step, yet success hides behind the next bend in the road. Never will I know how close it lies unless I turn the corner. Always will I take another step. If that is of no avail, I will take another, and yet another. In truth, one step at a time is not too difficult. I will consider each day's effort as but one blow of my blade against a might oak. The first blow may cause not a tremor in the wood, or the second, or the third. Each blow, of itself, may be trifling, and seem of no consequence. Yet from childish swipes, the oak will eventually tumble. So it will be with my efforts of today. I will be liken to the rain drop which washes away the mountain; the ant who devours a tiger; the star which brightens the earth; the slave who builds a pyramid. I will build my castle one brick at a time for I know that small attempts, repeated, will complete any undertaking. I will persist until I succeed."

-Og Mandino

BE PERSISTENTLY PERSISTENT TO SUCCEED.

Debunking Old Myths

Myth #1: *Only* those at the top make money.

Answer: Like *those at the top* didn't work to get to the top?

Myth #2: You got in at the beginning, so naturally you make the most money.

Answer: Those in the business in the beginning have made the mistakes that you can learn from. They are the pioneers. Learn from them instead of criticizing them. You have NO idea what it takes to start at the beginning of a company unless you are one of the first distributors.

A Message From Jan Ruhe

I was in at the beginning of my company. I started when the company was new, fledgling, poor management, no money, no track record, no name recognition, no leadership, no computers, no cell phones, no fax machines, and no sturdy packaging. Many distributors quit and couldn't put up with the disappointments. I am glad I did put up with them and navigated through them. I sold a product that I believed in and sponsored others to do the same. Those who got in early into a company helped to build the company. Lift those distributors up as pioneers. Learn from them. Take a serious interest in those who had the courage to stick with a company during changes and tough times. They are the champions. There were 200 other distributors in my company when I joined. Almost all are gone today. Not me, I stuck around for the payday. You should too.

HAVE STICKABILITY!

Develop A Champion Attitude

One reason distributors don't want to get on the phone is that they lack interest in doing what must be done to move the business ahead. Regardless of how much you want to achieve, unless you develop a genuinely positive attitude toward getting on the phone, you will not grow a Network Marketing business.

Build An Incredibly Positive Mental Attitude

* A positive mental attitude is the single most important principle of the science of success.
* Your mental attitude is the only thing over which you, and only you, have complete control.
* A positive mental attitude attracts opportunities for success, while a negative mental attitude repels opportunities, and doesn't even take advantage of them when they do come along.
* A positive mind finds a way it can be done...a negative mind looks for all the ways it can't be done.

Gotta Wanna Make Calls

Before you can build it big, there is something that must happen *inside* of you. You are in some way moved to take action to do what is necessary to achieve that which you desire. Without desire, most distributors are not going to move the business ahead, no matter what you say to them on the phone. It won't matter. For those of you who want to do the business, wild horses won't stop you. The bottom line is you gotta wanna build it big, build it fast and build it to last.

BUILD IT FAST!

Speak to others like you wish to be spoken to.

There is a gold mine in your goal mind.

Focus On Positive Results

In an interview with golf champion Jack Nicholas, he was asked, *"How many more majors would you have won if you had not missed a five or six foot putt in the last two holes of a major championship?"* He got so angry that he left the interview. He told the guy that he had never missed a four or five foot put in a major. They showed clip after clip where he had missed a short putt. He could not remember it. He would not allow his mind to focus on bad results.

Touch your business every day!

Share Success Stories

We buy and use many brands because we are intrigued by how they are made, their special ingredients or their history, etc. If you don't have a story, borrow one or tell a brief story about your company. Collect exciting stories. Stories sell.

FORGET PAST MISTAKES... YOU CAN'T CHANGE WHAT YOU DID FIVE MINUTES AGO.

The Future Is A Mystery

Take your future into your own hands. It's too precious to leave it up to someone else. Who knows what lies ahead in life? Take good care of your future, after all, you are going to be spending the rest of your life there.

Focus on your Future

Look forward to never looking back. The future is so bright you better wear shades. Your future is going to be massive.

The Easy Roads Are Crowded

"The easy roads are crowded and the level roads are jammed; the pleasant little rivers with drifting folks are crammed. But off yonder where it's rocky, where you get the better view, you will find the ranks are thinning and the travelers are few. Where the going's smooth and pleasant you will always find the throng, for the many, more's the pity, seem to like to drift along. But the steps that call for courage and the task that's hard to do, in the end result in glory for the never wavering few."

-Edgar Guest

Top distributors have a purpose; a sense of urgency; and they have the heart to pursue it when other distributors quit.

CHAPTER TWO
GET SERIOUS

Building a Network Marketing business to the top takes getting serious about working the business. There are those who talk about building a business, and there are those who will stick with you for years and never ever get to the top. You will have disappointments galore, but all of the tough years of building are the price you will pay for leaping past mediocrity. I was so serious about calling people that many times I got nothing else done in the day but making calls. I watch people who say they are serious and year after year they don't move their business ahead. I bet that if they tripled the calls they made the previous year, they would see progress. You can lead a horse to water…

The Fortune Is In The Follow Up

Network Marketing all boils down to thousands of distributors each doing a little bit, **often.** Everyone knows someone. Every eagle knows a sparrow. Start contacting everyone you know and spreading the word. The easy part is, the more you do, the faster your network will grow. If the fortune is in the follow up, is following up too much to ask to make a fortune? *The fortune is in the follow up.*

> *"I shall pass through this world but once. Any good that I can do any kindness that I can show any human being, let me do it now and not defer it. For I shall not pass this way again."*
> -Stephen Gallet

Speed Up The Process

Speed up building your business by using the phone *wisely* and to your advantage. Be *eager* to pick up new ideas for scripts, encouragement, powerful words to use, how to respond, how to plan calls, how to overcome objections and the best communication skills possible. Be a student of that which gets results and then take action and duplicate that which you have learned.

Be Your Own Best Customer

With personal experience of using your own product, your enthusiasm and belief will grow. If you are unenthusiastic about your products, why would anyone want them? Use your products.

Calling At A Concert Pitch

How would you like to sell and recruit all the time at concert pitch? When an orchestra plays at *"concert pitch,"* the hard preliminary work has already been done; the long rehearsals are over. Now, at the concert, the individual instruments fuse together into one harmonious flood of sound. Smoothly and powerfully the orchestra carries the audience with it. When you are selling and recruiting at concert pitch you are carrying your prospect with you, without seeming effort. You take them along with you, from benefit point to benefit point. You are in charge of the presentation, quietly and inoffensively. The presentation concludes with the prospect joining you, buying from you, or giving you a referral. What is so important, both the prospect and you have a sense of personal satisfaction, that the prospect has made a good choice and that you have a new sale, referral or new distributor. Make that call!

Who Are The Top Distributors?

Those who burn with an overwhelming fire of desire to prove something to someone succeed. There is no such thing as a natural born Networker. The great ones have been trained to be great.

Desire Sleeps...Wake It Up!

Desire Sleeps… it can be awakened by a movie, a lyric of a song, a presentation, a gift, a seminar, a distributor, a hostess, a sermon or a phone call. Wake yours up! Have massive desire... take action!

Ignite Your Passion

Today the buzzwords are *"know your why."* If you had asked me what my *"Why"* was when I joined, I would not have understood you. Use words and phrases the average understand. I knew I was going to succeed. No one knew my *"Why"* at the time but **an internal flame had been ignited within me**. When I joined, I got a new identity… a woman in business. I knew nothing of Network Marketing jargon at the time.

The Fire Of Intense Desire

* **Desire is infinitely more than just wanting or wishing for something.** Just because you desire to have something doesn't mean you will get it, especially if you take little to no action. It is more than compulsion or stimulation to achieve.
* **What is intense desire?** Intense desire is an overwhelming demand for change, a personal war with things as they are and the willingness to make any sacrifice to bring about change.
* **Desire burns like a white, hot flame in the heart of every person who strives to be successful.** Desire is the quality that makes winners in every walk of life. A person with intense desire makes commitments instead of promises; goes through challenges instead of going around them, and has the courage to say *"I'm good, but not as good as I should be."*
* **Desire urges people forward with insatiable appetites for competition, action, and all the successes the world has to offer.** There is an active self-awareness in intense desire. It gives its possessors the feeling that they have a mission to perform, a destiny to meet and conquer.

"Close your eyes, give me your hand, darlin'…Do you feel my heart beating? Do you understand? Do you feel the same? Am I only dreaming? Is this burning an eternal flame?"
-The Bangles

"People are motivated to do exactly what they decide to do."
-Edith Price Penniman

The Internal Flame Of Desire

Get people as excited as you are about your products and making some money. Don't get analysis paralysis and have to understand everything. Begin to dream big. You can make a go of your products as a viable business if you can sell enough of them. So, the journey begins. Start making the calls. When I first got started, I had a raw internal flame that was lit forever. Desire had been stirred, big time, by just someone making the call. Take yourself to the next level, not only have desire, but increase that desire to *intense* desire.

Develop More Will Power Drop the Won't Power

When you make up your mind to succeed in Network Marketing, follow through on what you say you will do. Don't allow your nerves to play havoc with you after you have made a decision. Once you have made the decision, stop worrying about it. Have more *will* power than won't power. Don't be average, be a champion.

Network Marketing Works

Have belief in Network Marketing. Believe in the promise that *if you help enough others succeed, you will get everything you want.* When you grasp how huge this opportunity is and how exciting it is to build something out of nothing and that your success is up to you, you will be anxious to get up in the morning and get to work. You will get up early, stay up late, and study what those getting massive results are doing.

> *The more calls I make, the luckier I become.*

LUCK Is Spelled W.O.R.K.

You can get lucky in Network Marketing, but it's not the norm. It boils down to hard work. There are three things that happen when you make the calls:

1. You become confident faster.
2. You compress time.
3. You literally develop momentum, which will carry you to the top.

Will Power beats Should Power!

If you don't want to make calls, you won't.

It's not how much you call.
It's the results you get.

The Power Of Enthusiasm

Many top distributors have attested to the power of enthusiasm in their business. In fact, there is so much power in enthusiasm that perhaps now we tend to disparage the excited distributor who preaches, *"be enthusiastic."* But to disparage enthusiasm is one of the costliest mistakes you can make. Enthusiasm is extremely important on the phone. It is the key to greatness in Network Marketing.

> *"I stayed fired up and so excited about the opportunity of Network Marketing that if everyone I recruited through the years quit, I would have built it all over again!"*
> -Jan Ruhe

Enthusiasm vs. Hype

When you are passionate about what you are doing, you can't help but be excited, over the top, buzzing with excitement, and wanting to share with the world the opportunity you have found. It seems too good to be true that there is a path in life in addition to or to replace 8-5 to earn a substantial living. Unleash your passion, speak with enthusiasm, and confidence, instead of feeling you are pushy or filled with hype. There is a power of true, sincere, enthusiasm, that once ignited, the flame can never be doused or put out.

TRIPLE YOUR ENTHUSIASM!

Ten Ways To Get Fired Up For Life!

Have a hopeful and confident attitude that communicates to prospects through the words you use and the way you say them. It is a willingness to express yourself in a straightforward way which will be contagious and lead to a productive and mutually beneficial exchange. You want your efforts and calls to lead to successful accomplishments of your objectives and spread to others who will be attracted by our enthusiasm. Here are ten specific things you can do to get yourself fired up to make the call:

1. Don't be afraid to laugh. It's the telephone equivalent of a smile.
2. Don't be critical or make disparaging remarks.
3. End your conversation on a friendly, hopeful note.
4. Express an interest in who you are talking with.
5. Give a sincere compliment right away.
6. If the call doesn't work out as you had hoped, treat it as a learning experience.
7. Let your voice show that you enjoy life. Sound happy.
8. Never argue with the prospect.
9. Psych yourself up before an important call.
10. Use Power Words (see page 99).

Powerful Knowledge Stimulates Enthusiasm

Learn more about yourself, your product, your opportunity, and your prospects. The extra knowledge will give you greater confidence and security. Your enthusiasm will increase in direct proportion to your knowledge of your opportunity.

Suggestions:

* Schedule periodic classroom sessions with yourself. Do this in your non-phoning time.
* Test yourself with questions about your opportunity, your product, your customers and yourself.

> *"Success is not a result of spontaneous combustion. You must set yourself on fire."*
> -Arnold Glascow

The Exciting Selling Season

And let's call it that from now on; we'll let the average distributors call it the *slow season*. The time of year when business is slower than other times has a number of big advantages for the distributor who will get on the phone and talk to prospects. You can offer lower prices. You can offer better service. You can talk to more people than you have time to in your busy season.

HAVE THE FIRE OF DESIRE FOREVER!

Enthusiasm Is Contagious

* **Enthusiasm is a state of mind.** It inspires action and is the most contagious of all emotions.
* **Enthusiasm is more powerful than logic,** reason, or rhetoric in getting your ideas across and in winning over others to your viewpoint.
* **Enthusiasm is to progress toward success as gasoline is to a car's engine.** It is the fuel that drives things forward.
* **Enthusiasm stimulates your subconscious mind.** By feeding your conscious mind with enthusiasm, you impress upon your subconscious that your burning desire and your plan for attaining it are certain.
* **Put loads of enthusiasm in your voice.**

Generate Positive Enthusiasm

There is sound psychological basis for the power of enthusiasm. Every distributor is subject to fears. There are fears of making the first call of the day, of the greeting from a tough prospect, to ask for the order, to ask the prospect to join you, and of not succeeding. One of the chief values of enthusiasm is that it replaces fear. Fear can be crippling; but when the emotional force of fear is used to generate enthusiasm, our fears disappear and become filled with positive power.

> *"High achievement is dependent upon your drive, enthusiasm, persistence, and on your extra effort."*
> -Chris and Alan Goldsborough

Unleash Raw Enthusiasm

I had no sales training. I was shy and had only raw excitement. Once I DID understand the possibilities, after six months in the business, I sponsored 13 distributors with no system, no upline help, and no company support. My point? If you wish to succeed and have little to no support, you can. Begin with raw enthusiasm, hope and the phone.

Enjoy Making The Call

* Be well-prepared. You will then be confident and with confidence comes ease.
* Realize that you will not get appointments or recruits from every call you make, no matter how good you are.
* Remind yourself to relax.
* Try taking a few deep breaths before you start calling. It has a calming effect and will help you speak properly.
* When you are relaxed when you make your phone calls, your tone is more conversational, your voice more natural and lively, and your attitude one of friendliness and optimism.

"When your work becomes a joy,
undreamed of possibilities open up for you."
-Medhi Fakhzadeh

"I just called to say I love you,
I just called to say how much I care."
-Stevie Wonder

Be Sincerely Sincere

The only people you will influence to any large degree will be the people you sincerely care about.

On The Phone:
50% Show Biz
100% Sincerity

Sincerity Pays Off Big Time

If your prospect feels that you are sincerely interested in helping them succeed, you stand a better chance to increase your recruiting results. You can show your sincerity over the phone in a number of ways:

* **Answer your phone and be available immediately.** Your attention will convince the prospect that you are truly interested in customer service and the prospect's time.
* **Make regular phone calls to the prospect.** You will assure the prospect that you are honestly interested in them, and that you want to help them to not only get involved, but to massively succeed.
* **Take the prospect's questions seriously.** Your frank attempts to give the prospect accurate information will express your interest in satisfying the knowledge they need to make a decision to join you.
* **Take the time and interest to ask your prospect about their needs and wants.** You will convince the prospect that you are genuinely interested in getting them into the business.

Enforce Self-Discipline

* If you don't discipline yourself, you are sure to be disciplined by others.
* Self-discipline is the process that ties together all your efforts of controlling your mind, your personal initiative, positive mental attitude, and controlling your enthusiasm.
* Self-discipline makes you think before you act.
* The subconscious has access to all departments of the mind, but is not under the control of any.
* Without self-discipline, you are as dangerous as a car running downhill without brakes or steering wheel.

It's A Big Numbers Game

Accept that Network Marketing is a numbers game. When you meet with a disappointment like rejection, a canceled appointment, or a stall, put it into the proper perspective by looking at it as a part of a game.

Move Products=Make Money

Through your career, you will make literally thousands of phone calls. There is only **one** way to make money in Network Marketing: move products out of the Warehouse(s) and into the hands of the masses. It's that simple. Don't complicate it. Those who make the most calls with positive results make the most money. Move massive quantities of product and you get a lifestyle most only dream of.

THERE IS A DAY YOU DECIDE TO BE THE BEST YOU CAN BE, MAKE THAT DAY TODAY.

Two Ways To Move Product

You can move massive quantities of products by:
1. Yourself, or
2. By enrolling, sponsoring or recruiting others to do the same. Every other way of reinventing the wheel is a waste of time.

A Large % vs. A Small %

You can only move so much product, kit cases, or re-orders, through parties, catalog, or online by yourself. The idea in Network Marketing is to recruit thousands of distributors each doing a little bit, often. Wouldn't you rather make 3%+/- off of millions of dollars/pounds/euros moved than 40%+/- off the efforts of yourself or in addition to your own efforts?

It's Simply Mathematical

Do the math…assuming you have 52 parties a year (if you do home parties), one a week with approximately 10 people at each party, you can reach 520 people in a year. Many top distributors talk to that many people on the phone a week easily. Talking with 520 people in a year is slow growth. You can talk to many more people on the phone in addition with your face-to-face prospects that will help you speed up the growth of your business.

Example: If you want to share your opportunity with only one person a day, you will talk to 365 people. To speed the growth up, simply talk to more people. Do the math on 20-30 phone calls a day or more, six days a week equals over 6,000 people in a year. Smart choice.

GIVE YOURSELF A RAISE, HERE'S HOW: GO INTO MOTION!

When you go into motion, that creates commotion and commotion creates **PROMOTION!**

Find Five To Reach Five

The idea of Network Marketing is to teach five distributors to each get five distributors and to teach them to do the same. The numbers grow fast when you do this and you can teach this in your phone calls from the very first call. Paint the picture of the money that can be earned on your own efforts and the efforts of others.

$$5 \times 5 = 25$$
$$25 \times 5 = 125$$
$$125 \times 5 = 625$$
$$625 \times 5 = 3{,}250$$

Each 3 Reach 3

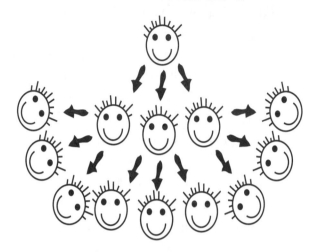

LET THE RECRUITING EXPLOSION BEGIN!
MAKE THAT CALL!

The actions you take today will pay off big time in a few years. So will the actions you don't take.

"PUT A TEAM TOGETHER, BY MAKING CALLS, LIFTING OTHERS UP, AND GUIDING SOME... UNTIL FINALLY YOU GET ONE HEARTBEAT, TOGETHER... A POWERFUL TEAM."

-Amy Nunnelly

Building A Future Takes Time

If you are worried about tomorrow's business, you are in deep trouble: If you are planning for customers two years from now, you will have plenty of business tomorrow. Nothing valuable happens instantly. Customers aren't standing in line at the front door of distributors' homes. The job is to sort through the public to find people who want to join your opportunity. Go to work on perfecting your phone skills.

Nothing Valuable Happens Instantly

When it comes to attracting new business, there are no magic tricks, no shortcuts, no *"easy"* ways, no get-there-fast gimmicks that always work. It just doesn't happen.

"Ours is a society that demands instant gratification. We want what we want and we want it now. Most real rewards, however, don't come that way. Usually, you must be willing to do the work, to give more than you are asked, before you begin to collect the interest on your investment."

-W. Clement Stone

Be Hungry To Make Calls

Be hungry and eager for financial security and know if you recruit enough people and teach them how to recruit, Network Marketing has to work.

A BIG SHOT IS ONLY A LITTLE SHOT WHO KEPT ON SHOOTING.

F. A. Y. C.

Forget About Yourself Completely!

Tune Into To WIIFM

What's in it for me? The prospect wants to know what's in it for them to join and the fact that something is good or great doesn't necessarily mean they want to have anything to do with it. Mention a benefit to the prospect first thing. Keep this *"you"* emphasis in mind no matter what methods you are using to get a prospect's attention.

Quit Talking About Yourself

One of the best things to remember on the phone is that as soon as you say the word *"I"* you can lose the prospect fast. Keep the focus on the prospect. As time goes by, you can build rapport and friendships that include information about you, but at the beginning of a conversation, keep the focus on the prospect.

Let's talk about Me, Me, Me is OUT in Network Marketing!

Interested Is Interesting

When talking to prospects on the phone, take an interest in *THEM*. Don't talk about you. Ask these questions and discover *their* values:

* *Are you happy with your lifestyle as it is?*
* *Have you ever been in Network Marketing?*
* *What do you like about it?*
* *What do you not like about it?*
* *What would entice you to join?*
* *What has to happen in order for you to feel...?*
* *What is most important to you in (life, investments, cars, family, security...)?"*
* *What is your level of commitment if you join?*
* *What would you alter or improve about what you have now?*
* *Where do you live? What do you like about living there?"*
* *Who in addition to yourself will make the final decision to get involved?*

> *"Nurture your mind with great thoughts for you will never go any higher than you think."*
> -Benjamin Disraeli

As you proceed with your questions, sprinkle in these questions rather than lecture the prospect about Network Marketing or your opportunity.

* *Did you know that...?*
* *Do you find it surprising...?*
* *Does it surprise you...?*
* *Don't you think that...?*
* *If I could show you a way...?*
* *Would you be interested in...?*
* *Would you like to see...?*

Imagine Making The Call

When you get on the phone, imagine that you are working on an assignment in preparation for a promotion. Envision your increased paycheck rewarding you for the outstanding work you are doing now. Allow your imagination to be creative; to take in all ideas, regardless of how wild they may seem at the moment. Stop only when your ideas no longer have any relationship to reality. Start thinking. Write down your ideas for future reference. Imagine people thanking you for calling on them because they were looking for a home-based business to join.

Cultivate A Powerful Vision

* Creative imagination has its base in the subconscious and is the medium through which we recognize new ideas and newly learned facts.
* Imagination recognizes limitations.
* Creative vision sees no limitations.
* Imagination springs from experience and reason; creative imagination springs from your commitment to your definite purpose. Make that call.
* Visualize yourself making the phone calls and your team growing. Your imaginative faculty will become weak through inaction. It can be revived through use.

You can't stroll to a goal! What are you waiting for?

CHAPTER THREE
GET READY

Big time success is about being totally committed and disciplined to talk to as many people as you can and as quickly as possible. It is not about being a trainer blabbing in the front of the room. It's about building a business that pays you residual income forever. Not only will you use the phone for prospecting and recruiting but also for training and leading your team.

What Are You Waiting For?

Many distributors never reach the top. Why? They think it's because of the prospects they didn't convince. But that's not the truth. It's because of the prospects they didn't talk to. If you want to get to the top, make the calls, and see next year's prospects this year. Don't procrastinate. Procrastinators are experts in creating alibis and excuses. There are reasons *why* distributors succeed and only excuses why they don't succeed. One excuse is as good as another.

Give Out Information In This Order

1. The benefits of working with you.
2. The support they will get from you.
3. The training you will provide.
4. The Pay Plan and the earning potential for the listener.
5. The products.
6. What comes in the starter kit.
7. How many people are in their area.
8. Where they can view you information online (or what you have to send them).
9. The company image.
10. The company management.

Take Urgent Action!

Call The Neighbors...Hurry!

Would you get on the phone to all of your neighbors if you saw some top distributors in your company arrive in your neighborhood to start canvassing for new distributors or would you continue to have analysis paralysis?

Make An Exciting Offer

Network Marketing is not a matter of *"landing"* a message. Rather, it is crafting your message carefully and accurately in terms of what the prospect is already thinking. We are not trying to change anyone's mind. Our job is to *"make an offer"* that coincides with the goals, objectives, desires or needs of the prospect. It is not what we want to sell that counts, but what the customer wants to buy that must occupy our attention.

"Increase your business starting today. Use this information. It has helped us build a huge business. Prepare for abundance."
-Mel and Irene Wilson

Shoes Needed Or Not Needed

There once was an owner of a shoe company in England who believed that his shoes would sell all over the world. The owner sent his top distributor to Africa to a native village to sell shoes. The next day a cable arrived to the owner saying that there was no business in this village, that there were 6,000 natives there and no one wore shoes. The owner summoned him back to England and soon sent another, less seasoned distributor to Africa to the same native village to sell shoes. The next day a cable arrived to the owner saying that there was astonishing business in this village, that there were 6,000 natives there and no one wore shoes.

Attach more fear <u>to</u> NOT making the calls than <u>to</u> making the calls

Create Personal Initiative

It is better to act on a plan that is still weak than to delay acting at all. Procrastination is the archenemy of personal initiative. Personal initiative is the inner power that starts all action.

Here is why to take personal initiative:

* It is contagious.
* It succeeds where others fail.
* It creates results.
* It creates opportunity.
* It creates the future.
* It creates advancement.

Business Is Everywhere

The top distributors see business everywhere whereas the average are talking about how slow business is and how hard it is to get started and to stay motivated.

LET THE GOOD TIMES ROLL!

Business is booming!

Start Spreading The News

From Frank Sinatra: *"Start spreading the news…I'm going to be a part of it…If I can make it there, I'll make it anywhere…it's up to you New York, New York!"* So it is in Network Marketing, **start spreading the news**…*I'm going to be a part of it…If I can make it there, I'll make it anywhere…it's up to you …*

Happy Talky-Talk

In the movie South Pacific the song was sung, *"Happy talky-talky happy talk, talk about the things you like to do, you've got to have a dream, if you don't have a dream, how you gonna have dream come true, if you don't talk happy and you never have a dream, then you'll never have a dream come true."*

You've Got To Have A Dream

At first, I had small dreams but they were my dreams at the time. Six months later someone *finally* shared with me the possibilities that Network Marketing could be much more… it could be my path to a new lifestyle. Prospects with priorities, hopes, needs, wants, and dreams will always succeed. Be eager to get on the phone to start spreading the news.

> *"If you want a harvest next season, grow a crop. If you want a harvest in ten years, grow a tree. And, if you want a harvest for a lifetime, grow people."*
> -Chinese Proverb

The Sorting Business

We are in the sorting business. Sort through the masses to find people who do want to join you. Build leaders and make them successful. It only takes a few distributors for your train to leave the station.

Just A Spoon Full Of Sugar

From Mary Poppins: *"Just a spoon full of sugar makes the medicine go down, in the most delightful way!"* The confident distributor does not back away when the prospect breaks into *their* presentation. Instead, welcome the exchange. Realize that this is the prospect's way of:

* Showing off their knowledge.
* Asking to be convinced that they are making the right decision.
* Sprinkle answers with sugar that everyone likes to hear. Here are a couple of key phrases:

Distributor: *"That's an excellent point, Susie,"* or, *"An observation like that makes it obvious that I'm dealing with a pro."*

Hint: The sooner you get busy contacting people on the phone, the faster your business will grow.

If It's Going To Be…

Deciding to get on the phone is your choice. You don't have to do it. No one can make you do it. No one can motivate you to get your phone out and start calling. You are not a puppet on a string. No one is going to make you do anything. Instead of fearing getting started, use the mantra, *"My rewards in life will reflect my service and contribution. If it's going to be, it's up to me."*

Does The Compensation Plan Always *Really* Matter?

You might think your Compensation Plan is *the very best* and no other company can compare. But if the prospect has no interest in selling your product, no interest in the opportunity, it doesn't matter what your Compensation Plan is. The Compensation Plan is only the solution to the fears and pains your prospects want to avoid or a ***way to get what they want.***

What Really Matters?

One call and a life is changed. I didn't know about the Compensation Plan, and if the distributor had told me about it, whatever she would have told me would not have mattered. Only what ***my hopes*** were mattered…can I make some money selling these products? What was important was for someone to show me a way to stay home with my babies, work my own hours, be my own boss, and a way to make money doing it on my own terms.

IT'S CRITICAL:

Remember to ALWAYS ask for referrals if your prospect is NOT interested.

Intend To Succeed

Many distributors think about making the call, want to make the call but do everything in the world *but make the call*. Be the one who makes the call. Intend to succeed.

Come From Contribution

You don't have to start with real talent. Talent is cheap. You can buy it, you can rent it, and you can buy a ticket to go see it. You don't have to have a PhD or a university degree. Education is not cheap. You can have a wall full of diplomas but fail at Network Marketing. The real achievers understand that our business is a people business. It's our attitude that is the criterion for success. You can't buy an attitude at any store, online or from anyone. Attitudes simply are not for sale! Get over yourself. Get you out of the way. Think of what you have to offer to others. Come from contribution, how can I make someone's life better?

Never Misrepresent Who You Are Or Your Company

If you sense resistance to your opportunity or product on the prospect's part, don't try to give the impression that you are selling something entirely different and then hope to dazzle the prospect in an appointment. A prospect who thinks that they have been tricked into giving you their time is an angry one and rightly so. The victim of this kind of deceitful approach will usually become aware of it and of course will then refuse to see you or talk again under any conditions. Companies have been torpedoed by this kind of trickery.

> *"The only thing that stands between a man and what he wants from life is often merely the will to try it and the faith to believe that it is possible."*
> -Rich DeVos

The Law Of The Farm

Building a business can be like running a farm. We till the soil, fertilize it, keep the weeds out, and make sure it is protected from bugs and bad weather. Some seeds will grow while others will wither. All we can do is water, fertilize and weed.

Law #1: Prepare the ground: Decide you are going for greatness and know that this is your own decision. No one can keep you motivated but you.

Law #2: Begin to Plant: Make the calls. Watch your deeds, they start with needs and can become seeds. Leads are seeds, so what deeds do you need to do to start a growing business?

Law #3: Nourish: Follow up. Explain your opportunity.

Law #4: Convert: Learn the words and closing skills.

Law #5: Not all seeds will grow: It's our job to plant the seeds. Sometimes the birds get some of them, sometimes the sun burns them up, sometimes the water washes them away, and sometimes they fall on rocks and can't take root. But all we need is a few to take root. Don't get discouraged. Press on.

Law #6: Not all leads turn into recruits: Don't fret about them. Some will join you, some won't, so what, there is always someone else to invite to take a look at your opportunity; someone is waiting for you to show up and make your presentation.

Law #7: Those who take root will grow: These will be your leaders. All you need is a few strong leaders.

Sow The Seeds Of Your Income

Your ability to plant seeds and tend your plants well will show up in the crops you will harvest. It's not actually about the number of calls you make; it's about the percent of the prospects you call who you actually meet or convert to a distributor that is the key to residual income. You can control that percentage as well. Learn to talk to all kinds of people. Seek strong seeds. The strong seeds will grow regardless of you. However, if you only bring in weak seeds to your farm you will be forever propping them up and hoping they will grow.

The Judge And The Jury

Phone calls are like making a presentation to a jury. In every call, your prospects are simultaneously judge and jury. When the presentation period has ended in the courtroom and closing arguments are called for, you, the distributor make your close and you ask for the sale. State your case!

> *"The truly persistent distributor struggles against overwhelming obstacles, overcomes call reluctance, labors in the face of sharp criticism and does what few if any understand."*
> -Dorothy Wood

Master Your Presentation Skills

There is much information to learn in *The Master Presentation Guide*. Available at www.janruhe.com.

Conquer Call Reluctance

Call reluctance is negative expectancy. It's when you expect everyone to be negative, reject you, hang up on you, yell at you, scream at you, give you a hard time, say bad things about you or something else horrible. Pretend you have an invisible remote control (like you use for your TV), and simply change the channel in your brain and watch another movie in your head. As long as you play a movie on your inner mental screen that nothing is going to work, or that it's too much work, or that you are too lazy to do it, that is what will show up in your belief system.

Overcome Call Reluctance

To overcome calling: **1.** *Want* to. You have to make up your mind to overcome this. **2.** *Believe* passionately in what you are doing and in your product and opportunity. We are in the business of helping people, not selling drugs or bothering people. When you believe you are helping people, then you do not feel as though you are bothering them or taking away from what they are doing. Change your mental movie.

Have, Do, Be

So many distributors think be, do, have. I have to **be** somebody, and **do** something, to **have** what I want. Actually, turn that around, if you become the person you **have** to be, **do** what it takes to reach your goals, and you will **be** everything you can possibly want in a lifetime.

Expect the Unexpected

First Impressions

You only have one chance. If you mess up on that first call, chances are you are finished with that prospect.

There is never a second chance for a first impression!

Benefits, Benefits Benefits

The main job of the call is to sell the benefits, to enroll people or set up a time to meet to share the information. Make sure the prospect *wants* to either talk on the phone or meet in person. The only reason a prospect will agree to a meeting is because they want the *benefits* to them. It is with *benefits* that you whet the appetite of a prospect once you have gained favorable attention.

Benefits To The Prospect

Concentrate on what your product or opportunity can do for the prospect, rather than what it is. Convey the impression that the benefits you describe can be theirs with a minimum investment and will require only a few minutes to explain.

Distributor: *"You will be amazed at how simple this business is to put it to work for you. You can start enjoying the benefits from the day you join or get happily involved."*

Remember: Wanting is an emotional state. The benefits that you describe should be aimed at emotional appeal. Focus on **wants** more than just needs.

Truly Appreciate Network Marketing

Appreciate Network Marketing for its mental challenges, the competition it offers, and the lessons of discipline, teamwork, sacrifice and life that it teaches. Building a business teaches you to get up and fight back after being knocked down. Network Marketing has never been a ho-hum business to me. I knew from the day I put pen to paper that this would be my career. It's kept me motivated because I never wanted to go back to the lifestyle of never having any money, and settling for a mediocre lifestyle was not an option.

Want To Succeed Forever

If wanting to succeed is a fault, as some of my critics years ago seem to insist, then I plead guilty. I love to succeed. I know no other way. It's in my blood. You have got to keep trying to succeed before you can succeed. Succeeding is a *"we"* thing, not a *"me"* thing. You must be working to succeed all the time, even though only a small number of things you do determine your success. You never know which things they are or when the chances are coming. I have been around a lot of distributors who want to succeed, but none as much as I did.

> *"There is a lot of blood, sweat and guts between dreams and success."*
>
> -Paul *"Bear"* Bryant

Don't Coach Network Marketing Coach People Skills

Stay Mentally Motivated

If you ask me what motivates a distributor or a team, what makes them keep going through thick or thin, I'll tell you, I don't have the answer. I do know for myself that I've been motivated from the day I learned about Network Marketing and what it could provide for my children. I stayed mentally prepared to make the calls all my career. I never gave up.

It's An Inside Job

There are two big forces at work, external and internal. We have little to no control over external forces such as tornados, earthquakes, floods, disasters, illness, terrorists, and pain. What really matters is the internal force. How do we respond to those disasters? Over that we have complete control. We cannot always control circumstances. But we can control our own thoughts.

> *"Like the waves of the sea are the ways of fate as we voyage thru life. 'Tis the set of the soul which decides it's goal and not the calm or the strife."*
>
> -Ella Wheeler Wilcox

ONLY YOU CAN MAKE A DIFFERENCE

Watch Your Voice Tone

All the seminars, books, CD's, Power Points presentations, and DVD's are useless if you have a voice that squawks, groans, is pessimistic, chirps, squeaks or mutters. Your voice tone matters.

Total Impact Theory Of Sales

Body and other nonverbal=55%

Voice (tone, pace)=38%

Verbal (words)=7%

Total Impact=100%

Total Impact Theory Of Phone Call Success

Concentrate much more on these two types of communication when speaking on the phone. They are all you have to offer:

Voice (tone, pace) =60%

Verbal (words)= 40%

Total Impact=100%

Verbal Communication

Network Marketing involves two-way communication; you talk directly to the prospect and, if you say the right things to arouse interest, the prospect will listen and talk to you. In most cases, you can't complete your presentation over the phone and, even more, you can't show the prospect what you are trying to get them to see to join you easily over the phone.

> *"Your activity will promote you or expose you."*
> -Michael and Sandra Laydon

Improving Your Phone Voice

Warmth: Warmth is hard to fake. You really have to feel it to project it.

Clarity: Emphasize all p, t, d, k, b, l, th, ch, sh, and sch sounds.

Enthusiasm: Enthusiasm is infectious.

Inflection: Imitate the professionals; listen to TV announcers and top radio speakers.

Sincerity: Come from how can you help someone else get what they want.

Volume: Lower or increase the volume. Don't talk too loud or too soft.

Enunciation: Don't slur your words or talk like you have marbles in your mouth. Work on having no thick accent.

Whining: Do not whine like a spoiled child.

Pace: Vary your pace, speed up your talking, then slow it down.

Don't Speak Too Loud

Years ago when we lived in Texas, I had a distributor in Alaska who would call me and YELL like she was yelling all the way from Alaska to the USA mainland. I told her I could hear her just fine and to please not yell. I actually had to hold the phone away from my head because she talked so loud. I made the suggestion to talk more quietly to her many times but she did not listen to me. It was not too long after that she quit the business. I bet people she called didn't miss her calls!

When in doubt, lower your voice.

Powerful Voice Tone Tips

* Be clear and enunciate words well to avoid possible misunderstandings.
* Be confident, use a tone of voice that expresses a can do attitude.
* Be courteous, helpful and sincere.
* Be interested and enthusiastic; let your voice say you enjoy what you are doing.
* Be warm, friendly and businesslike.
* Breathy sexy imitations have no place in your calls, nor do macho or Rambo type sound-a-likes.
* Come from contribution. How can you help the prospect? Not how can the prospect benefit you.
* Don't be too intense.
* Don't talk in a monotone; emphasize key words by moving up or down the voice scale.
* If you have a baby voice that never grew up and you think it's adorable, that's fine, but it could be a massive turnoff to a prospect.
* If you sound tired, speed up your delivery.
* If your tone of voice is too high, deepen it.
* Never call a prospect when you are upset. Let that upset pass before calling so that you are in control of your voice.
* Smile when speaking, and blink occasionally.
* Speak clearly. If you have a high voice, work HARD on lowering it.
* Vary your voice.

You Can't Take It Or Leave It

If you are sharing something casually with a friend or someone else, that can be considered Networking or just *"sharing"*. But when you are moving product for compensation suddenly the motives change and you will begin to approach the business differently. Once you get serious about Network Marketing, you don't want to share casually and you don't want people to have a take it or leave it attitude. Now, you will CARE about what happens, because now you have a financial interest.

> *"Seize this very minute; what you can do or dream you can do, begin it. Boldness has genius, power and magic in it. Only engage and then the mind grows heated; begin and then the work will be completed."*
> -Goethe

> *"It's a funny thing about life; if you refuse to accept anything but the best, you very often get it."*
> -Somerset Maugham

ALWAYS REMEMBER TO SMILE

Our Company Doesn't Sell

The average distributor insists: *"I am not selling, my company doesn't sell, we just show the products and share and care about people. I heard someone at a seminar say we are not in sales, and that's who I am going to believe."*

Note from Jan: Bye bye, those who continue to be embarrassed by being in sales… you will never get to the top. Pay attention to **sales** techniques, they will help you build your business.

Are We In Sales Or Not?

Anytime that you exchange a product for money it involves sales, persuading, sharing, and communicating. Let no one dupe you into thinking something is wrong with being in sales. **Sales is the greatest industry on earth.** Don't let anyone knock sales. *It's so fun* to sell products and opportunities that people actually want. The average people get hung up on the words *sales* or *retail*. They don't want the stigma of being a *"salesperson."* But you must get past that and be proud to be in sales. **We are in sales**, no matter what speaker comes to tell you or tries to persuade you differently. **CLEARLY**, they have never made it to the top in Network Marketing. The incredible amount of distributors who join that do nothing before they become discouraged, are simply convinced Network Marketing is not sales. Get clear, **we are in sales.**

Why The Hesitation?

Distributors are not nervous or hesitant to share about a movie, a restaurant or a sale at a store, so why the hesitation when they join Network Marketing?
Answer: Because it's not just sharing, and when you are in Network Marketing, **you have to learn selling skills.** That is uncomfortable at first because you believed you were not selling anything, especially if the pied piper comes along who has NOT achieved in Network Marketing and that's their message. Whenever someone tells you we are not in sales, you can be sure they never made it to the top of Network Marketing.

We Need People Like You

Many listen to those who do NOT understand the power of Network Marketing and say, *"In our company we do not sell."* They fervently believe this myth and they do as they are told. They do not sell. All selling involves is demonstrating or presenting products and sharing the opportunity. The idea is to sell our products and opportunity to others. We need people like you to help us do that.

Distributor: *"Our products do not sell themselves; that is why we need you to tell as many people as possible and tell prospects how they can become distributors too. We will teach you how to do it so that it is easy and enjoyable. We need people like you. Come with me, let me show and tell you how easy it is when you represent our company with our products."*

"The idea is to build a massive, thriving and successful business. Get started by making phone calls today. Take urgent action. Your future starts today."

-Elise Vermilye

CHAPTER FOUR
REACH HIGH

Network Marketing is the greatest industry in the world. As in life, some people travel, others wander, and still others unfortunately simply escape. Life is a game of choices. There are no timeouts. The clock keeps ticking. Decide today to build your business no matter what, stay resolved, to make those calls, to go forward and to take the journey to the top. Decide to make this year the finest in your life. Get out of the stands and get on the field of life. Life is not a spectator's sport. You have to be a player. The time to start is now. Never ever give up. Make one more call.

Do today what others won't so you will have tomorrow what others don't.

"Treat people as if they were what they ought to be and you help them to become what they are capable of being."
-Goethe

EARN WHILE YOU LEARN!

How A "Bad" Salesman Sold $1 Million A Year

Dave Bellizzi is the perfect example of how the numbers game will make you rich: *"When I first started selling insurance on the phone, my sales manager pointed out to me a man and told me that he had the worst approach and worst sales presentation he had ever heard."* And he added that this man was one of the top salesmen in the company. Every year, his sales were well over $1 million. The man would dial a number out of the phone book. When somebody would answer, he'd say, *"You don't want to buy any insurance today, do you?"* That's awful, a completely negative approach and didn't go along with the Sales Manager's system. But this man didn't want to conform to the system. So, he made loads of calls. Most people would answer *"No"* and hang up. He kept calling dialing one number after another. Maybe one person out of 100 would say *"Yes."* The thing was, that person he met with would buy. Why were his sales so high every year?

Because he was calling 300 people a DAY, 6 DAYS a week. That's 1,800 calls every week.

He was serious about making money. He never complained. Only eighteen people would listen to him and some of those people had medical challenges and would get turned down, but he sold enough insurance to make The Million Dollar Club in his company. Then one day, he learned about asking for referrals and he increased his sales significantly. He used the same approach: *"You don't have any friends who want to buy insurance, do you?"* It's a numbers game. Worked for him.

50 Important Phone Rules

1. Always search for ideas that you can use on the phone to increase your business rapidly.

2. Avoid wasting time waiting on the phone while being put on hold by someone. Ask the prospect if calling them back would work better for them. Even if you save yourself ten minutes a day, that is lifetime you can't get back.

3. Be a self-starter.

4. Be a visionary; look into the future of what your life can be like through your own efforts of making the calls.

5. Be happy to work the business on the phone. Be driven to work the business on the phone.

6. Be highly self-motivated to get on the phone.

7. Be proud to be in sales. It is the greatest industry on earth. Be proud and eager to make sales and opportunity calls.

8. Believe that you can make more calls than you are making, even if you never have before.

9. Call when you think you can reach the prospect. This isn't as difficult as it seems. If the prospect you are trying to reach is someone you do not know, call between 8-10am in the morning or before 9pm in the evening. This way you might catch them. It's better to actually contact a prospect than to keep leaving messages.

10. Come from contribution. Work from the premise of how can you help someone else succeed.

11. Constantly be contacting new prospects; at least twenty prospects a day.

12. Do not be denied success. You must make the call.

13. Do not demand that your spouse work the business like you do on the phone. Show them the way and let them be creative and use their own talents. There is no one-way to do this business.

14. Do not neglect your family by being on the phone constantly. Others are watching you. Is this the message you want others to get? Instead, spend quality time with those you love.

15. Do not tolerate wimpy distributors who are not willing to prospect, make the calls, and follow up.

16. Do what you must do and gain confidence by being in control of your lifetime. Make more calls. Talk to more prospects.

17. Don't blame the weather, the economy, your family, the terrorists, the company, the Compensation Plan, the upline, a natural disaster or an unsupportive spouse or partner for your lack of success so that you don't get on the phone.

18. Don't let anyone kill your dreams.

19. Don't waste time calling back prospects that really are uninterested. It's a waste of precious lifetime.

20. Get on with making the calls, even in trying times.

21. Have a sincere desire for the people you talk to.

22. Have the vision that success is yours when on the phone.

23. Help others by telling them the benefits of what they can accomplish working with you.

24. Invest monthly in the greatest investment on earth, your mind.

25. Keep your phone calls concise, so that the prospect can quickly hear what you want them to hear. Lengthy phone conversations are passé.

26. Keep your phone call uncomplicated. Ask the prospect during your call if they are *"with you,"* or are *"following you,"* or if they have any

questions. Do this throughout your call, not at the end.

27. Keep your sense of humor. Phone calls can be fun!

28. Keep your word. Return phone calls when you say you will.

29. Know that rejection is a part of the process of sorting through the public on the phone.

30. Know why you are calling the prospect and what you want to say. Be prepared. Have specific information at your fingertips. This will save you and your prospect time. You certainly wouldn't think of fumbling through your briefcase or handbag during a live presentation, so don't do it over the phone.

31. Know your math. When a prospect asks you what the current investment is to get involved and what they get for that investment be accurate.

32. Live in the present moment and keep your enthusiasm for your vision for the future. Always paint the picture of what the future will look like working with you and being a part of your company.

33. Love people and use money instead of loving money and using people.

34. Make as many calls as possible during one stretch. Why? This will put you in a groove and you won't have to interrupt yourself from some other important duties during the day.

35. Make follow up calls and make the calls promptly. Have a follow up system.

36. Make sure your voice is clear.

37. Make the commitment to overcome fear and prepare to succeed.

38. Mind your own business. Don't take time to gossip.

39. Network Marketing IS sales. Period. Do not let anyone tell you that Network Marketing is not sales. It is. Distributors move products that people purchase. Whoever tries to tell you that Network Marketing is not sales is totally ridiculous and clearly has NEVER succeeded in Network Marketing.

40. Never EVER make a call before 8am, EVER. Unless this is to a close friend or family or that you have an appointment set up prior to the call.

41. Prospect more than anyone you know.

42. Radiate confidence and strength in your belief as you convey your opportunity on the phone.

43. Selling principles apply to printed material just as it would during a phone appointment.

44. Stay focused on the task at hand.

45. Strive to keep your life in balance in all areas including financial, personal, physical, mental and spiritual. During some parts of your climb to the top you might be out of balance and that is okay.

46. Take your future seriously. Make more calls.

47. The more accurately your benefits fit with your prospect's wants, the more likely they are to give you the time of day to listen to your presentation. Making the call to follow up is like an uninvited guest and the only chance of you being welcomed is to hit on the benefits the prospect would like to have.

48. Time is money. Make the most of your time. You wouldn't sit in a prospect's office indefinitely, so why waste time on the phone?

49. To make calls that will get the prospect's attention, be prepared.

50. Watch your voice tone. (see page 36)

Mind Your Phone Manners

* Ask for 5-10 minutes of the listener's time.
* Ask if it is a good time to be making the call.
* Don't hang on the phone too long.
* Don't share everything that you are doing with the prospect. Most don't care.
* Don't say your company name as if you were ashamed of it. Be proud to represent your company.
* If someone isn't interested, ask for a referral.
* If the prospect is totally not interested, thank them for their time and move on.
* Just as appearance and other personal details are important in the actual interview, the personal impression you make on the phone is important, too.
* Keep your mouth close to the mouthpiece.
* Speak distinctly and loudly enough to be heard.
* Think and sound cheerful and optimistic, no matter what the reaction on the other end has been.
* Use a conversational tone, as you would in person.
* Your first ten words are the most important to establish the purpose of the call.

Avoid These Irritants

* A nervous laugh.
* Begging someone to join you or to listen to you.
* Chewing gum.
* Clearing your throat or coughing.
* Clicking over to call waiting. Never put the prospect on hold.
* Forgetting to ask for referrals.
* Noisy backgrounds.
* Putting people on hold.
* Putting your hand over the mouthpiece so that you can converse with someone else while the prospect is talking.
* Smoking or drinking something between phrases or sentences.
* Staying on the phone too long.
* Stopping to fuss with or at or answer your children.
* Talking about yourself.

Never assume. . .
It can make an Ass out of U and Me.

Make That Call!

Ass.u.me

You Bore Yourself

Making thousands of calls can get boring at times. Keep your sense of humor. Have contests with other distributors on how many calls each can make in a certain time frame that get results.

Respect Those You Call

Here is how to respect those you call:

* **Timing:** When you have something important to talk about, ask the other person to pick a time that best fits THEIR schedule rather than expecting them to bend their schedule around yours. If you need to talk right away, and they say it's not a good time, honor their concern instead of forcing the issue. Let them know the exact amount of time you will need and make the commitment to not take any more time than is mutually agreed upon.

* **Respond and Validate:** Be sure to respond to the other person and validate their legitimate feelings, opinions and concerns before moving to your own agenda. If they say something that you believe is incorrect, rather than abruptly correcting them, say, *"I can see why you might think that, but you should also know that..."* Anytime you take notes on what is said or you positively comment on something they say, you show that you believe their opinions are worthwhile, and respect, honor and trust are built.

* **Respect the talker:** Commit to show respect to the person you talk to. **Treat prospects with respect.**

* Work hard to **convey respect and consideration.**

"At the end of every day, when you really think you've done everything you can to move your business forward... make just one more call."

-Andy and Claire Stephenson

Six Benefits Of The Phone

The phone can be one of your most important sales tools, if it is used properly. Here is what it can do for you:

1. It enables you to get an idea of the prospect's potential of joining you or wanting your products.
2. It gives you a preliminary personalized contact that will increase your business.
3. In some cases, it gets you to a person whom you would not be able to see merely by stopping into an office.
4. It quickly and inexpensively establishes a time for a definite interview or appointment, without wasted traveling or waiting.
5. You can ask for referrals easily.
6. You can contact a lot more people than you can prospect during the day face to face.

Make Calling A Top Priority

I got the children off to school and raced home to get on the phone (before cell phones). Cleaning the house was not a priority, building the business was. I was not a maid. I was an entrepreneur, and I knew it. I had the vision of a gorgeous house and a lifestyle for my children. My vision of a better life kept me going. I was not going to settle for mediocrity. The main priority is to learn phone skills, increase your vocabulary, paint the picture of Network Marketing over the phone; and to be ready to recruit someone as soon as they give you the green flags that they are ready to join. You will learn this by making a lot of calls. Nothing, absolutely nothing takes the place of experience. Start today!

Full-Time Commitment vs. Partial Paralysis*

When you crystallize your thinking about building your business, you will make a full-time commitment. *Full-Time Commitment* enables you to focus your attention on the activities necessary to bring your hopes and dreams into reality. Until you are willing to make a *Full-Time Commitment* to your own success, you will be handicapped by partial paralysis. *Full-Time Commitment* frees you from obstacles and roadblocks that otherwise limit your success. Those with partial paralysis will make a few phone calls and give up easily. Not the Committed. They persevere.

With Full-Time Commitment

* You are confident about the future because you know where you are now, where you are going, and how you will get here.
* You are eager to begin each day's work.
* You contact your upline regularly to discuss progress toward your goals.
* You know exactly what you will do each day.
* You make phone calls with enthusiasm.
* You welcome objections because they give you the opportunity to make sure that the prospect understands the opportunity completely.

Learn from the mistakes of others, You can't live long enough to make them all yourself.

With Partial Paralysis*

* You are worried about the future because you have no idea what it holds for you.
* You begin the day shuffling papers or drinking an extra cup of coffee while you decide what to do first.
* You dread each day because it is overloaded with too much to do that you really don't want to do.
* You dread objections because you see them as a rejection of you personally and you can't spare the extra time to deal with them.
* You have ups and downs but the *"up"* times get further apart and the *"down"* times last longer and longer.
* You hope your upline doesn't contact you because you have nothing to report.
* You immediately quit for the day when a presentation does not produce a recruit so you can recover from the feeling of rejection.

*adapted from Paul J. Meyer

Crystallize Your Thinking

Total success demands total commitment. Crystallize your thinking by deciding to pursue your dreams, visions, hopes, desires and goals with *Full-Time* commitment. Pay attention to your thoughts. What you focus on is what you are going to get.

100% Commitment

You cannot merely *give it a go*, you cannot say you are 98% committed. How would you like your spouse/partner to say that about your relationship? How would you like your surgeon to be 60% committed to operating on you? There is no such thing as 110%. There is only 100% when you decide to go to the top of Network Marketing.

Three Drawbacks Of The Phone

The phone has three serious drawbacks that can kill a Network Marketing business before it gets started:

1. It is easier for many people to say *"No"* over the phone than it would be if you were talking to them in person. For this reason your presentation must be well planned and well executed to get positive results.
2. The impersonal nature of the phone dismays some distributors who find that they are less able to cope with objections and unexpected challenges on the phone than they would be in a personal give and take situation.
3. Many distributors misuse the power of the phone. How? Simply by turning a sales/recruiting call into a social call and wasting valuable prospecting time.

Practice, Drill and Rehearse

When you start thinking about what you are going to say on the phone and you have a plan, PDR (**P**ractice, **D**rill and **R**ehearse) your presentation. Ask someone you trust to critique you to listen to you practice. Practice in your car, in the shower, take a walk and say your presentation out loud. The more you make your presentations, the more you will perfect them to get the results you want.

Avoid Caller Burnout

Caller burnout is a reaction common to some distributors who spend much of their day on the phone. At its extreme, burnout is characterized by an inability to take a break.

Suggestions to keep from burning out:

* Avoid cold drinks and any beverage with caffeine in it.
* Call someone you love every day.
* Don't smoke, smoking will only aggravate vocal problems caused by stress and also you could get a smoker's cough that is a distraction to those who don't smoke.
* Lubricate your throat with lukewarm water at regular intervals.
* Take mini breaks and stretch your legs often.
* Take time to look outside while you are on the phone.
* Take time to take a walk.

Take Short Breaks

Plan time off for short breaks from constant phone calls. You have to take a break from phone presentations. Plan for these breaks. You don't want to burn out. If you are sitting, get up, take a short walk, visit with your family. It may only take a few minutes but it will help you be more successful.

Principles Of Effective Calls

* Prospecting on the phone relies more heavily on what words we say and the way we say them than those presentations we give face to face.
* Be positive on every single call. Word travels.

Carefully Plan The Call

Carefully plan what you have to say and say it. Write it out and then read it that way over the phone. This eliminates awkward hesitation, forgetting or repeating anything and it adds assurance to your words. It will have spontaneity if you read the words carefully each time. Develop your phone conversation requesting an appointment along these lines:

* Identify yourself by name and your company name.
* Tell the prospect why they would benefit from listening or meeting with you.
* Ask prospect for an appointment to explain the benefits of joining your team.

The Learning Curve

As with any repetitive task, the more often you repeat the task during a continuous block of time, the better you become. Prospecting is no exception to the rule. Your second call will be better than your first, your third better than you second, and so on.

Go To The Prospect

You can go to the prospect or you can try to convince the prospect to come to you. The hard way is trying to get them to come to you. Prospect by advertising, referrals or word-of-mouth. This can be costly and, to some extent, time consuming and wasteful. Only a tiny percent of the people you try to reach will actually take the trouble to contact you. So, if it is at all possible in your business, don't rely on customers coming to you; you go to them.

YOU ARE THE STAR!

The Seven Main Call Objectives

What do you want to achieve or avoid? The answers to these questions are your *objectives*. How will you go about achieving your desired results? The answer to this you can call *strategy*. The main objectives we use the phone in Network Marketing, are to:

1. Sponsor new distributors.
2. Sell products.
3. Train and empower others.
4. Keep in touch.
5. Make announcements.
6. Share and care.
7. Set up appointments.

"Can you think of anything more permanently elating than to know that you are on the right road at last?"
-Vernon Howard

The Four Stages Of The Call

Even in the shortest, briefest call, lead the prospect through these four stages:

1. **Capture attention:** Your opening must get attention immediately.
2. **Contact Information:** Make sure that you leave your phone number, even if the prospect has it in their caller-ID.
3. **Follow Up:** Let prospects know that you will be following up with a phone call about any information that you sent them.
4. **Use *"You"* Emphasis:** Don't talk about yourself. Talk about what the *benefits* are to the prospect. Quit talking about yourself.

Five Main Questions To Ask

These five powerful questions are the most important questions you will ever ask in prospecting.

The Rules:

❋ The order must not be changed.

❋ After you ask a question, you must remain completely quiet until you hear the answer.

❋ Use the prospect's words to feed back to them what they have told you.

The Questions:

1. *What would be your number one reason to join Network Marketing?*
2. *Why did you pick that one reason?*
3. *Why is that important to you to achieve?*
4. *What are the consequences of not having that opportunity or worse, not working your Network Marketing plan to get what you want?*
5. *Why would that worry you?*

Prospect: *"None of them."*

Distributor: *"Well if one reason were to be **the** most important, which one would it be?" Next, shut up and listen."*

No Time To Waste

You will probably speak less than a minute in making an average prospecting call. *The first ten words out of your mouth are the most important.* That gives you little time to waste, and since your whole purpose is to make the prospect curious enough to give you some time on the phone or an appointment, get to the point as soon as possible. Unless the person is a friend, avoid pleasantries or generalities; get to the point.

Get To The Nuts $ Bolts Fast

Get to the *"Nuts $ Bolts"* the minute you start your call and you will see your sponsoring climb.

Sponsor-losing statistic: Most distributors talk twice as much as they should and say half as much as they could. Don't dominate the prospect by dominating the conversation. Let the prospect participate in the conversation. Get to the specifics by following these suggestions that will help you to get to the prospect wanting to join you.

Top Nuts $ Bolts For The Call

❋ **Start with something special.** Make your products' benefits seem like exclusive benefits.

❋ **Watch out for *"positive"* boredom**. Prospects tend to become bored with the distributor who asks simple questions that only demand a token *"yes"* or *"no"* response.

❋ **Ask the prospect questions introduced by what, how, why, when and where questions.** These are questions that can't be answered by a simple *"yes"* or *"no."* This allows the prospect to talk and tell you what his needs are. Doing this keeps the listener involved in the conversation and considering your opportunity.

❋ **Keep questions brief.** Questions you ask a prospect should be short and simple to answer. Know the exact point you are going for and then hit that point sharply and crisply. Any question over twelve words is too long.

Network Marketing Works - do you?

The First 30 Seconds

* **Smile:** Even if you don't feel like it, smile. This will ensure that you sound friendly.

* **Introduce yourself and, very briefly, your company:** Be very careful how you enunciate your name and the name of your company. Since you know what you are saying and do it all the time, don't get sloppy and say it in a way that is unclear for someone who has never heard it before.

* **State the reason for your call, including the benefits:** Do you talk with strangers if they don't say why they are calling? Probably not. Tell the prospect you call how they will benefit from the call.

* **Ask if this is a good time to talk:** If not, get a commitment to call later at a specific date and time or within a specific time frame.

* **Don't respond negatively** if your prospects are *"short," "cold,"* or *"annoyed."* Do you like people to call you about buying a product or service? Most people don't. Visualize the prospect who answers as engaged in some pleasurable activity or conversely as being upset in life. Avoid feeling rejected or angry if they are abusive in some way. Stay friendly and appeal to them to help you with your objective.

> *"But by the books you read and the people you talk to on the phone, you will be the same person you are today in the next three years."*
> -Charlie "Tremendous" Jones

Setting Up Appointments Tips

If you want to actually meet with a prospect here is what to do:

* **Suggest a time:** Unless you do, you are forcing the prospect to think of a time, which is bothersome to some people. Not only suggest an hour and day, but also ask them to advise you of a more suitable time if your suggestion is inconvenient for them.

* **Hint:** If for some reason the date you suggest is the only one which would be convenient for you (for instance, if you can be in their area only on a certain day), tell them that. Under such conditions many prospects will have the courtesy to arrange to be available at that time if they want to see you, or at least they will let you know if they *don't* want to meet you then.

* **Point out that there is no obligation to join.** With some prospects, this assurance can make the difference between giving you the appointment and not doing so.

* **Make it easy to join your opportunity:** Don't have too much paperwork. Go on and fill in any paperwork that you can and make sure you have a pen with ink in it.

* **Make sure you get a commitment** that they are going to meet you. Ask them to reconfirm. This will save you the time that you go to meet someone who had no intention of meeting you but could not be honest and tell you so.

> *"The secret to my success is that I bit off more than I could chew and chewed as fast as I could."*
> -Paul Hogan "Crocodile Dundee"

CHAPTER FIVE
BE THE BEST

Top distributors set very high goals, goals that are so high they can only be reached with the help of others. If you are to become a high achiever, you must be willing to settle for nothing less than reaching your full potential.

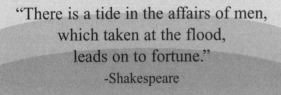

"There is a tide in the affairs of men, which taken at the flood, leads on to fortune."
-Shakespeare

Think Like A Billionaire

Donald Trump says *"Billionaire's don't take vacations."* When you love what you do, you will stay connected and in touch. I remember skiing down Aspen Mountain and stopping to check my answering machine to return calls right away from the mountainside if necessary. Get voicemail and check your messages while you are away and stay in touch. You never want to miss a potential recruit's phone call. Stay in touch even while you are traveling.

What Could Happen

What would your future look like if you get committed to make 50,000 phone calls to speed up your success? If you knew, without a doubt that making that many calls would increase your income so much that you could reach your outrageous goals, would you get up earlier and make your phone plans? Would you make more calls than you are making today?

I Bargained For Life

"I bargained with life for a penny, and life would pay no more. However I begged at evening, when I counted my scanty store. For life is just an employer, he gives just what you ask; but once you have set the wages, why, you must bear the task. I worked for a menial's hire, only to learn dismayed, that any wage I had asked of life, life would have willingly paid."
-Anonymous

The Voice Mail Presentation

Do you remember the days when a real live person used to answer the phone, when people actually used the telephone to talk to each other? Today it seems that we spend more time speaking to voice mail than to real people. Most distributors see voice mail as a necessary evil, something we put up with and give little thought to. But if you think voice mail messages you leave don't matter, think again. Voice mail is an important first impression of your professionalism, but is something that leaves many distributors tentative. Once you leave a message, you can't take it back.

Your Own Answering Message

Although you might think it's cute to have message from your children, it could be a turnoff for the prospect. *"Hi you have reached the home of Susie and Stephen Creamcheese and Sally, Sarah, Suzanne, Sophie and the home office of Susie with the Happy Dance Company, please leave a message."* **Remember, you are in a business.** You want no distractions to the caller. No children on the answering machine, smart choice. Make your message upbeat, alive and fun! Get voice mail: Have a separate number for your business.

Get a Private Line

For families who all use the same phone number you will want to get your own phone line for your business.

Do Not Have A Silly Message

Don't record a silly, unprofessional message.

No More Than One Company

It's not a good idea to put more than one Network Marketing business on your answering machine. Do NOT put on your answering machine to *"Press #1 if you want Susie with The Happy Dance Company or #2 for David who is with the Poodle Care Company."* Your callers will then know that you are not really serious about the Network Marketing business you are in and that you might be a part of another company. Not smart. Separate the two. Get another phone number.

Voice Mail Is A Golden Opportunity

Putting thought into messages you leave is very important. Voice mail is a golden opportunity. Use this moment of undivided attention to advance your opportunity. Voice mail can be a great time saver.

No More Than Four Rings

Some distributors let their phone ring and ring and will lose prospects fast that way. Answer your phone, or have it answered in four or less rings. Be available quickly to respond to a potential recruit or prospect.

Leave A *"Brief"* Message?

Don't you want prospects to leave a message of ANY length for you?

> ## Please leave a message of any length.

Seven Tips For Mastering Your Voice Mail Technique

Here are tips to use voice mail to your advantage.

1. Attitude: Make sure your voice conveys the right attitude. Smile when you are talking, stand up, get dressed up and do anything else you can to put yourself in a *fired up* frame of mind. You will feel more confident, your voice will come across stronger and you will increase your overall voice mail success.

2. Prepare: Preparation is the key to every professional task. Formulate and write down one line about what you would like to see accomplished with the voice mail message. What is your overall goal? What do you hope to get out of leaving this message? How can you get the most out of leaving the message?

3. Get facts: Get all the information you need for the call before you call. Have important information, your schedule, and contact information or anything else you might need to rely on ready while leaving the message. This will save you from fumbling noisily through a stack of papers and leaving a message full of *"ums"*.

4. Think message through: Organize your message into sequence of topics in the order of their importance. You never know how long you will be able to talk, make sure you know the most important information and present that information at the first of the call. Lead with your name and contact number. That way, if the prospect only hears ten seconds of your message, they will at least be able to know how to call you back.

5. Ask for a specific action: Leave the prospect a clear message about why you are calling. Make your message specific and clear. Make sure that there is no confusion left from your message.

6. Plan to call back again: Some people leave one voice mail message and think that their work is done. This is a mistake. Many prospects don't respond to every message in a timely fashion. Let prospect's know that you understand their busy schedules. For example, end your message by saying, *"I know that you are very busy, so if I do not hear back from you by Tuesday I will call you again."* This eases the other person's feelings when they are not able to call back, and gives you an opening for calling again.

7. Conclusion: If there is a way to wrap up your business with a voice mail message, do it. That way, you and your prospect can cut down on the time spent playing *"phone tag."*

8. Setting up an appointment: If you are setting up a meeting leave a message saying: *"I will meet you at 3:30 on Thursday at the Bistro. If I do not hear from you, I will assume that you I can count on your being there."* This approach can save you and the prospect a lot of time.

Sample Message

Don't get upset if you get voice mail. Many people screen their calls today. Leave a message saying, *"Call me back, I have some exciting news!"* If they are interested, they will call you back.

I HAVE EXCITING NEWS!

Teach Your Children Well

I was on the phone constantly when my children were growing up. When Ashley was a baby, I put her cradle by my desk and she started her early life right beside me while I made the calls (before cell phones). I would put a timer on in the kitchen and would tell the children that if they played quietly while I was on the phone, that when the timer went off, that I would take them to the park. We could not afford cable TV in the early years, and there was no such thing as videos or DVD's. They simply played as children do. I never, not even one time broke a promise to them. In the early days, we went to the parks in a used station wagon that my grandmother bought me. Later, I took them to parks in limos. Before cell phones, I was never on the phone in the car. That was my time to listen to tapes on selling techniques and music and to talk with my children. Your children will learn along with you.

Who's The Parent? Who's The Child?

Many average prospects use their children as an excuse. *"I can't be on a call, that is the time my child gets home from school." "I can't be on a call then, that is when I help my child with their homework." "I can't be on a call then because my child is going to a sleep over at that time." "I can't be on a call because that is when I must meet with my child's teacher." "I can't be on a call then because I am going on a field trip with my child." "I can't be on a call that day because it is a school holiday and my children will be home."* Be different. If there is an important call coming up that you might learn something, make sure you are available. Have the attitude that you're doing this *for your children's future.* Arrange your day and time to be on an important call. Take your business seriously. Teach your children to behave while you are on the phone. You are the parent after all.

"Make your children WHY you make the calls."
-Kim Atherton

"It's not a job, it's a way of life."
-The Lady of the Rings

Be A Big Success Story

If you keep calling people and focus on building a Network Marketing business, you can become an *outrageous* success story! Only those who make the calls, loads of calls that get results, get to the top. When you are discouraged, pick up the phone and make more calls.

Be Totally Self Motivated

It takes a determined, self-motivated distributor to get to the top in Network Marketing. Self-starting power will put you far ahead of others who waste valuable phone lifetime by postponing their calls. Here are guides to help you build your self-starting power:

❋ **Begin immediately.** Don't waste your time waiting for a vague impulse or someone else to get you started. Right now is the time for you to begin.

❋ **Avoid putting-off.** If you procrastinate, you will disrupt your schedule and lose valuable time on the phone.

The top bananas get the most light.

Be Busy Giving Recognition

The more people you give recognition to, the more it will come back to you. If you are hungry for attention, the smartest thing you can possibly do is to be so busy giving recognition that you don't need it. Almost everyone is vulnerable to praise, and the prospect's vanity can be used as the target for your opening words. Use these words: *"When a person reaches your level of responsibility he has one thing in common with successful people in any business: life time is extremely valuable and simply has to be conserved. Don't you agree that five of your valuable minutes would be a good investment if over the phone I could show you how you can make some additional money each day, week or month?"*

Warning: False compliments must always be avoided. If you feel that the prospect will not like someone who flatters them, don't compliment them.

Duplicate Top Distributors

You will succeed if you duplicate top distributors who handle the phone with great success. Don't reinvent the wheel.

Hint: Set a goal to be THE top distributor in your company. The reality is, someone will be, it might as well be you!

Be the most successful distributor you know!

Success Stacked Upon Success

Your progress toward your goals should be steady and consistent. Each new level you reach becomes a new standard for your continued achievement. Success stacked upon success. Your progress toward your goals should be steady and consistent. Each new level you reach becomes a new standard for your continued achievement.

Power Phoning

Work daily from 8am-2pm and 3-6pm with no breaks, a quick lunch, no eating on the job, just hard driving and smart work. Only exceptions are appointments with potential recruits or emergencies.

Eye To Eye

Even today, with the Internet and the phone, the best way to really make an impact is to meet face to face with prospects when you can. Remember, we are in the people business. Just a packet in the post/mail might not be enough. Make the call and follow up.

Establish Clear Expectations

It is a colossal waste of time to beg someone to join you. Most likely they will do absolutely nothing and even taking time with them was a waste of time. Instead, ask questions and establish clear expectations of what you expect before you recruit them. Your expectations could be that you expect them to be on teleconferencing classes, to come to a training, to attend a conference or a convention or to return your phone calls. Make your own list.

Powerful Communication

* **Be considerate:** Many times people reject what we say, not because they agree or don't agree but because they are reacting to an offensive attitude that is projected by the talker. When someone perceives that you are being condescending or inconsiderate, they will put up defenses and close their mind to you and your opinions. They will focus on how fast they can get away from you. When you are inconsiderate this lowers self-esteem and fuels fear, frustration, hurt, anger and ultimately brings resentment upon yourself.

* **Getting the Big Picture:** The best way to have a successful conversation is to ask questions.

* **Preparation.** The more important the information that you wish to communicate, the more preparation you need to do before the presentation. What could the listener's opinions be, what are their objections or excuses, their hopes, dreams, visions, goals and fears and challenges. Prepare for important conversations. Don't waste your time preparing for unimportant conversations; it is a waste of your lifetime.

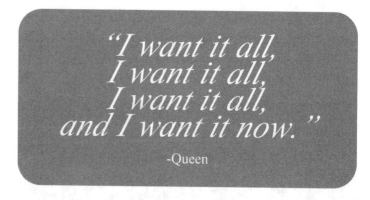

"I want it all,
I want it all,
I want it all,
and I want it now."
-Queen

Use Follow Up Systems

Use an Answer Book (see page 106) and use the Booking Letter (see page 83). The phone is not a heavy ten-pound weight but instead, it is a tool to use on your path to a new life. If your upline has a system that has gotten results, for goodness sake, copy it. Get an uncomplicated, easy system (see page 123). Get a spiral notebook or a grid-lined paper or use Excel. Identify some topics and get busy making the calls. If you don't have a system you might lose track of what prospects have said. Capture notes and review your system every day.

Use Systems Already In Place

There are many variations of systems and you have to experiment to find the ones that are best suited to you and your business. Whatever system you finally choose, make sure you use it regularly and consistently. At first it can seem like an awful nuisance. That's because it is something new. But if you stick to it and make it a regular habit, it will become second nature to you. Don't, whatever you do, fall into the trap of saying, *"Oh, I'm too busy tonight. I'll make twice as many calls tomorrow night."*

The One-Night-A-Week System

Many distributors use, successfully, the One-Night-A-Week System. They select one evening a week to make calls between the hours of 6-8pm. There's one thing better than the One-Night-A-Week System and that's the 2-Nights-A-Week System and that's twice as good.

The Better-Half System

Some distributors put their spouse or partner to work making the calls for them. One wife earned herself a full-length mink coat in less than two years, merely by making appointments for her husband. For each appointment that resulted in a sale, her husband gave her a fee for her service. The extra money her husband made as a result of this enabled him to take her to the kind of places where she could wear the mink. (Mink doesn't have to be the goal, how about diamonds, a Ferrari or Porsche, charity donations, or world travel too!)

The Two-Five System

Many distributors, before stopping calling for the day, make 2-5 more calls. In the 2-5 System, remember these numbers are minimum quotas. *"No answer"* doesn't count. They must be completed calls. Make sure they are all legitimate prospecting calls and not other business calls you didn't get around to making during the day.

Three-Way Calling System

When you first sponsor someone, make sure to ask them who are twenty people they know who might like to hear about the opportunity and join as well. Ask them to get you their names and phone numbers and then set up a time with the new recruit and three-way call the prospects. Let the new recruit listen to your words, hear you get rejected and watch you press on. You can help build a team under your new distributor fast. It works!

S.C.O.R.E. Strategy System

The more you call, the more you score. Success in Network Marketing is a numbers game.

S=Self-Starter: Be willing to sacrifice and discipline yourself and make the calls. No one can make you make calls. You must be a self-starter.

C=Concentration: You must concentrate. All distractions are equal. It doesn't matter what the distraction is, doesn't matter whether it's family or whether it's fun or whether it's sports or whether you're going through a divorce or you're sick, it doesn't matter. If you are distracted, then you are not concentrating. The consequence is that your business will not grow as fast. If you allow your concentration to be split, then you are not practicing the first rule, which is self-discipline. Get rid of all distractions.

O=Optimism: You absolutely must believe you will achieve. If you're to call someone, you better believe that they are going to become involved with you. At the end of your presentation, you have got to say, *"Give it a try!" "Join us."*

R=Recruit: The bottom line is you want to sponsor new distributors and train them to do the same.

E=Enjoy: Relaxing is different from enjoying. Relax is relax, just relax. The "E" is to enjoy it while you do it.

The Twist System

The **W**ay **I** **S**ee **T**hings. You might have to try some new things. It's always too soon to quit. Change your thinking. This is the way you see things now-twist it around and look at it differently.

The C.A.S.C.O. System

* **C**reate the prospect by making them realize a need.
* **A**rouse interest by creatively finding the motive or benefit that means most to the prospect.
* **S**timulate desire by creatively building the desire for the benefits.
* **C**onvince the prospect that the benefit will work for them by the quality of your presentation.
* **O**vercome objections by offering the prospect a new idea.

Make Elevator Calls

Call prospects and other distributors on your team and give them a lift. Just a quick call or a nice message can help distributors take their business to the next level. Do not just rely on email to keep in touch with your team. You have no idea how your distributors value hearing from you.

S.C.O.R.E.

> *"You pay a price for getting stronger.*
> *You pay a price for getting faster.*
> *You pay a price for jumping higher.*
> *But also you pay a price*
> *for staying just the same."*
> -H. Jackson Brown

The Prospect Cannot See You

There are distributors who are skilled in face-to-face presentations but seem to change when they get on the phone. They lose their effectiveness and are somehow different and less at ease. If this is you, remind yourself that many of the behaviors that work well for you in face-to-face communication apply to phone communication as well. Here are a few:

* Be certain the physical setting where you conduct most of your calls is a place for effective communication. If it is not, change it. Don't have noisy distractions and interruptions.
* Be *other* oriented, not self-oriented. Use the word *You* more often than *I.*
* Communicate for the future as well as now. Relationships often shift and change in unpredictable ways. A less than exciting prospect can turn out to be your best distributor. Conduct phone exchanges expecting that they will be long-lasting relationships.
* Time is money. Keep your calls brief.
* Understand the purpose of each call you make.

Hurry! Follow Up! Hop To It!

A phone call can perform a very valuable service besides arranging a time for an appointment; it can sell the appointment. If you have an excellent conversation, the prospect will not only expect you to follow up but will also welcome your call. Don't let the prospect wonder what happened to you.

> *"Sooner or later, those who win are those who think they can."*
> -Richard Bach

Find Reason To Join

No one sponsors anyone unless the prospect has a specific need to join. This infallible rule—that behind every recruit exists a reason to join, can be a miracle key to guide you to more profitable recruiting. Motives vary from prospect to prospect. One has a different motive from another for joining. When you accurately discover why someone wants to join you, you have found the *"heart"* of that person's values and goals. The prospect's motive or desire to join wants to be satisfied. Your presentation can then aim to satisfy this desire to join and lead your prospect into the fire of desire of getting started in your opportunity.

Focus On Prospect's Motives

While on the call, focus your attention on listening to the prospect's motives. Discover **why** a prospect might be interested in joining using this list. So easy! A specific opportunity usually appeals to only one or a few of the ten reasons people join. Armed with the answer to the question: *"Which motive (or motives) does my opportunity satisfy?"* You can formulate a successful presentation around your opportunity benefits that best satisfy those motives.

Primary Motivating Factor

Once you discover the prospects PMF and how to light a fire under them, you've found the key. Find out what prospects really want and what pains they want to avoid getting it. It's about *their* hopes, dreams, visions, desires and fears.

17 Top Motives To Join

Not everyone's PMF (Primary Motivating Factor) for joining is the same. You may find one or more on this list that are your PMF. Focus on these:

1. Desire for admiration from others (pride, prestige).
2. Desire for amusement.
3. Desire for comfort.
4. Desire for gain.
5. Desire for gratification of some appetite.
6. Desire for safety and security of self dependents.
7. Desire for saving of time, trouble or worry.
8. Desire for self-improvement/personal development, (boredom with current friends and acquaintances, job, knows they can do better).
9. Desire for utility or use value.
10. Desire for wealth (profit, economy, saving, financial freedom, retirement, pension).
11. Fear of loss.
12. Leaving a legacy (making their children proud of them, proving to someone that they can succeed).
13. Making a difference/helping others.
14. Meeting new people.
15. Need to love and be loved.
16. Owning own business (no boss).
17. Time freedom (more spare time).

Find Primary Motive

One or more motive is dominant in the prospect's mind. If it should be different from the one or ones around which you have built your prepared presentation, your job is to find the particular motive and adjust your presentation to meet the reason the prospect is interested in joining. Here are ways to do this:

* **Ask direct questions.** Try using the direct question method to find your prospect's motives for joining your opportunity. If you realize that you are on the *"wrong track,"* immediately begin to tell the prospect how your product will satisfy their needs and they will be in a more receptive mood to listen.

* Use the *Trial And Error Method* **to find your prospect's major motive.** The alert distributor uses the *"trial and error"* method to determine a prospect's strongest motive. Use your best judgment in the selection of benefits to present and then listen carefully for the actual words the prospect uses. This technique is a continuing process. As your company launches new products you can go back to the prospect and let them know about them so that this new information might appeal to a different motive.

Be Prospect-Conscious

Don't just look for prospects, create them. You have to, for if you don't, you won't recruit and build a business. With each person you meet, you are creating a prospect. Never hesitate to mention your opportunity and product to everyone you meet.

CHAPTER SIX
LEAP FORWARD

Each new day we rise and have a brand new day, we can use it anyway we wish. We can make more calls than anyone else we know. We can trick people into thinking we are making calls. But only we know what we are getting accomplished. If you will make calls, if you will quit watching TV, quit playing computer games for hours, sleeping late, spending time with people who are going nowhere, you can change your future more than you can ever dream possible.

Listen To Yourself

Listen to what you will say on the phone, and find the path that works for you so that you can teach others how to duplicate your system.

Talk Less, Listen More

Spend 80% of your time listening, 20% talking.

Being The Listener Gives You Advantages

When you listen, you won't talk too much. You will spoil the effectiveness of your presentation if you prolong it by unnecessary chatter. Your prospect's questions and comments, even objections will tell you where you have hit the target and where you have missed and why.

You Can Increase Excitement

To get someone to listen to the opportunity, you must overcome their fears and get them to focus on all the *benefits and pleasure* they will receive by becoming happily involved in the business with you. You can do this over the phone. Just talk, talk, talk about benefits to the listener! If you hear yourself talking about you and using the words *I, me, mine*, you are not going to have great results helping the prospect overcome fear. Attach more fear to NOT making the call than to making the call!

Arouse Immediate Interest

It is best to explain exactly what you want to talk about. Here is an example: *"Hi Susie, this is Jan Ruhe with The Happy Dance Company. I met you at the gym (or wherever) and wanted to call and share with you what I am doing and want to see if this might be of interest to you too. Could I have 5-10 minutes of your time to explore the opportunity with you, please?"*

Spark Interest From The First

Save the facts until later in the call or for use during the appointment. Don't just start blabbing. Wait, listen and see if there is interest or if the time is right.

Grabbing Prospect's Attention

Inject your message right into the top of the prospect's mind. There are hundreds of thousands of other messages competing for attention with your message. You want to believe that the message you choose to send will rise above all other messages and land at the top of the mind of someone who, ten minutes later, will call you instantly with a big order or want to join you.

Hook The Prospect To Listen

To hook the prospect into listening:

* Have a strong, captivating opening statement.
* Have a personal reference.
* Ask questions that cannot be answered, *"fine," "yes"* or *"no."*

LISTEN
LISTEN
LISTEN

> *"While on the phone, I listen carefully to what the prospect says AND take notes on what they say. This helps me to pinpoint how getting involved in our company can work for them. Then, while still on the phone, I simply help the prospect see how they can get involved in our business on the level that works for them."*
> -Anita Hand

Hooking Prospect's Attention

Hooking grabs the person's undivided attention instantly. Attention spans are like roller coasters. They go up, level off, turn away, go down, turn another way, go back up and then go back down. Attention levels rise, fall and wander. People are busy and many will listen to you for the first few seconds and hastily decide they are disinterested in a caller who seems to be attempting to get them to spend money. Only a good opening can induce people to listen to your information carefully enough to be convinced by it.

Remember: Many distributors are out recruiting and trying to make appointments with prospects. A good opening in your call could be the difference in a prospect joining you and might even have them excited enough to join on the call.

Do Not Interrupt

Do not interrupt and don't instantly correct any incorrect statements. Don't quickly change the subject from what they are talking about to what you want to talk about. Wait until they feel you have really heard what they wanted to say before you move on to what you want to say. As you listen to them, keep your attention visibly focused on them.

Active Listening

What does the listener think about the opportunity? How do they feel about it and why? LISTEN to them. Really listen.

May your network be like the capital of Ireland... always Dublin!

Salt Your Presentations

* Salting holds the person's listening attention level high throughout the entire presentation. Salt makes you thirsty. Always use this technique right before you make an important point. If you notice that your listeners are starting to lose focus, throw a little salt into your conversation to make them thirsty again. The more salt you add, the thirstier they will become for the information you are going to share with them.
* Create curiosity about what you are going to say before you say it.
* Only use as much salt as you need.
* Don't over salt. Too much salt is irritating and offensive.
* Salt by asking questions, giving a description or telling a story.

Distributor: *"Oh boy, do I have something exciting to share with you! Tell me how you are doing before I get into this exciting news!"*

No one will really listen to you unless they understand what you say.

Listen to your voice, would you listen to you?

Listen in to conference calls and teleconferencing classes taught by those who are fired up and who are getting results.

Drive-Through Listening

How many times have you placed an order at a drive-through window of a fast food restaurant or bank and had to go back and forth with the person inside? They repeat your order and don't get it quite right. You listen. Then you repeat it back to them, trying to correct the misunderstanding. You keep repeating and re-repeating your request or order and the listener finally gets it right. Do the same in conversation. When someone has an opinion, repeat it back to them. They are then very likely to correct any misconception you may have. You then repeat back again what you think they said and they will either say, *"That's right,"* or they will give you a corrected version. In a matter of minutes, you will understand what they said and they will know that you value them enough to have patiently worked with them to understand their point of view. Then you make your point and ask them to repeat it back to you and keep the drive-through talking going until there is mutual understanding.

Listen And Copy

Listen to those who are getting results or have gotten results on the phone and duplicate their words AND their attitudes. The sincerest form of flattery is for someone to copy you.

Listen and Respect

During the conversation, rather than instantly giving your point of view, listen attentively to their point of view.

Many people hear without listening.

Listen For Joining Signals= Green Flags

❋ **If the prospect starts asking a lot of questions view that as a Green Flag to continue on:** *"That's one of several points I would like to explain when we get together."* Or, *"You will get a much better idea from seeing what we are doing than just from hearing about it."* Or, *"So far, would you be interested in looking into this opportunity?"* or as you get more confident, then say *"It sounds like you are ready to get started, let's go ahead and order your kit. The next step is"*…and go into your close.

❋ **If the prospect starts using words that give you a signal from their words, you must be quick to recognize this and try a close immediately:** *"I suppose," "I wish I could," " It looks good," "If I could," "Maybe I will," "I ought to," "Perhaps I should."*

❋ **Most prospects want some reassurance they are not doing the wrong thing. These words really mean:** *"Mr./Mrs. Top Distributor, you don't think I am making a mistake doing this do you?"*

Listen to the green flags that you hear:

Don't Be Average, Be A Champion!

Listen Carefully For Values

Whoever is talking is expressing their **values.** With the right questions, we can allow the other person to give us the clues we need to lead them to the right decision for them. Listen for values. Once you discover what prospect's value THEN turn your presentation to exactly what THEY value. Listen for values, ask questions, listen, and overcome objections, go into your close. The more you listen for values, the faster your closing skills will improve.

Speak To Prospects' Values

Values are emotional states we believe are the most important for us to experience or to avoid. Values are different for each person. Humans are motivated by the desire to achieve or avoid various feelings. Some feelings are more important to us than others. If a prospect is not joining you it could simply be because they fear that joining you may be more painful than not joining you. The more you learn how to listen to prospects and to communicate your message effectively on the phone, the faster your Network will grow.

Listen To Prospect's Voice

Listen to the voice of the person who answers the phone. If they are excited, match that excitement; if they are quiet, mirror that quietness; if they sound rushed, be thoughtful and ask if this is a good time or would another time be more appropriate to call them back.

Listen For The Prospect's Frame Of Reference

The prospect has opinions, feelings, preconceived notions, biases, personal agendas, and misconceptions, past hurts, disappointments, failures, hopes, goals and fears. Listen and they will give you clues.

Listen For The Prospect's Ego

The listener may think they are smarter or better than you in your particular area of expertise.

The Prospect Would Rather Be The Speaker, Not The Listener

Many presentations are missed because the listener is busy thinking about what they are going to say instead of listening to what is actually being said.

Listening skills are as important as speaking skills during the call.

Let The Prospect Talk

The prospect *must* get a chance to talk or they will have every right to resent your complete monopoly of the conversation. Be sure that your presentation includes ample listening time. On the call talk, ask and answer questions.

Prime The Pump

Years ago people had to get water out of wells. There were pumps at the well that had to be primed to get the water flowing. Many times you had to pump the handle several times to get the water flowing. Some gave up after just a few tries, when the very next person walked up and pumped only one time and the water would begin to flow. Some give up too early in Network Marketing. Be the one who makes the calls.

Don't Prejudge

It takes all kinds to make this work. Don't prejudge. Every eagle knows a sparrow and every sparrow knows an eagle.

You Cannot Change Anyone

You can't change anyone; you can only choose how you wish to react to them.

Have A Reason To Call

Call the prospect and tell them of a new product or exciting launch. If your company doesn't have one, make up one and run your own special. Collect information about birthdays or special occasions and email or call customers and remind them about your product.

Popular Product Month

Contact your prospects each month and leave a quick message saying that your company has just put a product on special for the month and would they like to stock up. Give them a sense of urgency of why to buy or to get involved. Make up a reason to call your prospects.

JOIN US FOR A LAUNCH!

Call And Invite Prospects To Meeting

Call prospects and tell them that you would love for them to come to a launch of a new product. Explain what a launch is, such as, unveiling a new product.

Distributor: *"I am going to have some prospects over to check out some new products that our company has just launched, would you like to come... looking forward to your coming."*

Distributor: *"Everyone needs to bring at least one person to the meeting. It can be a prospect or new recruit. You are going to be excited about the information you are going to get!"*

Exciting Expansion Contest

Call prospects, friends, relatives and tell them you are participating in an expansion contest and ask who do they know who might be interested in another part of the country or world. Call it an *"Expansion Contest."*

"It's better to be a lion for a day than a sheep for life."
-Sister Elizabeth Kenny

Get The Scoop

Distributors love to hear company scoop. If you don't have a voice mail system, make sure that you use a teleconferencing company and set up quick calls to spread the great news.

Create Your Own Packet

If your company does not offer you advertising assistance, create your own. With imagination you can think of other types of mailings, post cards, samples, catalogs, recruiting brochures or any thing that will smooth the way for your approach for the follow up phone call.

Get busy making more calls. It's a way faster track to success and less expensive than printed material.

Weaknesses Of Printed Material

Your printed material might just happen to arrive on a day when the prospect is preoccupied and will hardly do more than glance at it. Unlike a phone call, a letter or printed material is out of your control once you mail it. When the conditions surrounding its arrival are not favorable, even the best information might be overlooked and then your follow up phone call is more difficult. Don't think putting out flyers and sending out packets is all it takes. You must get on the phone.

Suggestion: Follow up, and when the prospect does answer the phone, always ask if it is a good time to talk. If it is, rock and roll. Be prepared.

You never know what is going on under someone else's roof.

No Messy Packets

Through the years, distributors in all different companies have sent me packets of their information to review. Guess how many followed up? None. Zip. Zero. Their packets told a lot about them. They were a mess. Papers going all different directions, some with coffee stains on them, most without their names on them. I was amazed because I thought these distributors would have wanted for me to see their packets and be proud of them. Remember, your first impression is important. No messy packets!

"When the student is ready, the teacher appears."
-Tom Hopkins

When To Follow Up On Printed Information

Send out only as much material as you can follow up on. Timing is important. You can't afford to let a prospect wait too long before you contact him personally, or the effect of the mailing will be lost. Unless you normally canvass heavily by mail, warm up on only a few prospects at a time. If you send out printed material, plan to follow up on the phone within two days of it reaching the prospect.

IT'S CRITICAL:
Remember to always ask for referrals if your prospect is NOT interested.

Jog Your Memory

Before the day of the computer, there were phone books called Yellow Pages with thousands of names and phone numbers in them. They were laid out in alphabetical order and distributors could flip them open and start at the letter A and start a memory jogger list. Most everyone could remember people to prospect that they had not thought of before. There is also a Memory Jogger list in the book *Go Diamond.* Available at www.janruhe.com.

Don't wait to call a hot prospect

A List Of 100 Prospects

It can be helpful to create a list of 100 people and get new recruits to start calling to involve them in the business. Exit your house and begin face-to-face prospecting and spreading the news about your business. Put out more catalogs or flyers and talk to more people. Ask for referrals. Use S.T.E.A.M. Sometimes the list of 100 works faster if you help the new recruits with phone skills or let them listen in to how you prospect on the phone. Just to make a list of 100 and start calling really doesn't seem to get anywhere fast. Start with S.T.E.A.M. Train your distributors what to say on the phone! Don't just have them start calling without knowing what to say.

Leads are only hot for 24 hours!

The Big Question

How long should you stay motivated to stay on the phone to find five distributors and then to teach those five distributors each to get five distributors?

The Big Answer:
For as long as it takes!

The S.T.E.A.M. Method

Much of Network Marketing success comes from referrals. You must be known for what you do. The word STEAM is a great word to keep in mind while on the phone. If someone tells you they are not interested in your opportunity, ask them these questions and be prepared to write down names and phone numbers.

S. *Who is someone you know in **S**ales? Who sold you your car? Who sold you your house?*

T. *Who is someone you know who is a wonderful **T**eacher or personal **T**rainer?*

E. *Who do you know who is filled with **E**nthusiasm?*

A. *Who do you know who has a positive **A**ttitude?*

M. *Who do you know who needs to make or would like to make some extra **M**oney every month?*

KISS=
Keep It Simple and Smooth

Get Prime Prospects' Contact Information From Customers

How you ask your satisfied customers for names of prospects often determines the results. What you want to avoid is the answer, *"I can't think of anyone right now."* Make your request for prospects in terms of the qualifications that fit your product and you'll get your customer thinking harder for you.

Distributor: *"Who do you know who might be interested in my opportunity?"*

Prospect: *"I can't think of anyone right at this time."*

Distributor: *"That's only natural because you are probably trying to think of someone who is interested in buying toys (or whatever your product is). The women I am looking for are between 18 years old and grandmothers, love children and want to work from home. They have just had an addition to the family, are tired of their job, need some extra money, would like some new friends, or need some fun in their lives. Who do you know who fits into that picture?"*

Promoting Your Network Marketing Business

Get your name and contact information out in your area and across your country. Be known for what you do. Have people think of you-keep in touch.

Take this job and love it!

Smart Way To Use References

Some will not object to your using their name as a reference, if you ask for that privilege. The mention of a name as a direct reference provided the person is someone, whom the prospect knows and thinks highly of, is an effective appointment getter. The effect of the reference will be increased if you get the prospect to say that he knows the person who gave the reference.

Distributor: *"Susie, you know David who works in the print shop right up the street?* (Wait for answer).

Prospect: *"Yes, I know David."*

Distributor: *"David suggested that you could benefit in the same way that he has from my product or opportunity. Let me show you how it can be of help to you too."*

If You Continue To Do What You Have Always Done, You Will Continue To Get What You Have Always Gotten... Is it enough?

The Definition Of Insanity:

To keep on doing something the same way, expecting different results.

Are You Oyster Shucking?

Suppose that you are now a professional pearl hunter sitting on the dock by the sea. Every hour I give you a bucket of 100 oysters. Among the 100 oysters are five oysters that have pearls in them. The other 95 are empty. As a professional you take out the first oyster, cut it open and find it empty. You then, carefully, put it back together, hold it between your hands to keep it warm and then sit there for days, hoping it will grow a pearl. Is this what you would do? *Of course not!* You would throw the empty oyster away and reach in the barrel for another and then another, until you found the one with a pearl. Take urgent action. You know success is there for you. Don't keep on doing activities that are getting you nowhere. If there is no chance that you can find a pearl doing what you are doing, change what you are doing.

Always Be Planning Two Years Out

If you are worried about tomorrow's business, you are in deep trouble; if you are planning for prospects two years from now, you will have plenty of business tomorrow. Gather thousands of referrals. Don't stop with a handful of leads. Go for greatness!

"The barriers are not erected which can say to aspiring talents in an industry, "Thus far and no farther."
-Ludwig Van Beethoven

CHAPTER SEVEN
STUDY PEOPLE

Make a list of what you are willing to work for. Share it with your family. Display it on your desk, carry it with you, and refer to it often. Only put on this list what you really want. Be careful what you wish for as you might just get it.

Your Own Phone Personality

To be proficient at phone use, you must first identify your own phone personality. This test is a self-inventory that will identify those things you do well and not so well. First, assess your own personality to see how it affects your current phone communication. When you assess yourself you will be ready to making a change in attitude and behavior that will improve your skills.

Work On Your Personality

The ideal personality has the ability to change and adapt to relate to all types so that they radiate a warm, but powerful personality, which is magnetic. Start paying attention to people you don't like or don't communicate well with. There is something about you that can be changed to improve your skills.

Your Personality Affects Results

Each time you make the call you bring to that communication your own unique personality. It is not like anyone else's. Be aware of your personality and how it may affect your results. Answer the following questions about your personality as you think it is now. Compare your answers to the *"ideal"* answers that follow. Then, take **the Phone Personality Test**. (pages 70 & 71)

Listen For Personality Traits

Prospects vary as individuals in their personality traits. Attempts have been made to catalog various *"types"* of prospects and to set forth the technique that the distributor should adopt as each are encountered. None of the systems are completely right, because none of them make allowance for fluctuations of temperament in any one person. Although someone might be correctly described as a specific *"Personality Type"* that person at different times can display different temperaments.

Work harder on your personality than you do on anything else.

> *"No matter what you are today, or what you have been, you have the potential to be what you want to be."*
> -John Curtis

> *"Associate with people of like mind who share a common vision."*
> -William E. Bailey

Pay Attention To Test Results

To the extent that your answers differ from the ideal answers, you will have to work harder at developing your skills. Consider this exciting and a challenge. It is never too late to acquire new skills.

Personality Assessment Test
Answer Yes (Y) or No (N)

1. Do you think of yourself as an introvert?
2. Do you usually allow others to do the talking because you are reluctant to speak?
3. Do you think other distributors have better ideas to offer than you?
4. Do you think of yourself as an extrovert?
5. Do you seek out the company of others?
6. Do you encourage conversation with others?
7. Are you receptive to other points of view?
8. Do you offer new ideas willingly?
9. Do you dominate conversations?
10. Do you feel your own ideas are best?
11. Do you enjoy persuading others to accept your ideas?
12. Do you think of yourself as having healthy self-confidence?
13. Do you consider yourself to be a good listener?
14. Do you consider yourself a courteous person?
15. Do you consider yourself to be a well-organized distributor?

The Ideal Answers

1.	No	6.	Yes	11.	Yes
2.	No	7.	Yes	12.	Yes
3.	No	8.	No	13.	Yes
4.	Yes	9.	No	14.	Yes
5.	Yes	10.	Yes	15.	Yes

The Phone Personality Test

There is a possibility that you must change to a specific focus on your phone skills. The most successful distributors are those who know the demands of a particular skill and adopt strategies to meet those demands. To help you do this, take the test that follows. This test will give you a much better understanding of your present telephone habits. There are no right or wrong answers. Answer the questions honestly, keeping in mind that the first answer that occurs to you is most likely to be the one to choose. The idea is to identify where you are weak and begin to work on the skills to improve.

Answer the questions:

Always, Sometimes or Seldom

1. Before making an important call, I jot down the points I wish to discuss in the order I wish to discuss them.
2. I identify myself immediately at the beginning of a phone conversation.
3. When making the call, I first ask if the prospect has time to take my call.
4. I answer my own phone when possible before or during the second ring.
5. I am courteous to everyone I call and thank them for taking my call before the end of the call.
6. I listen with empathy to the prospect and attempt to come from contribution.
7. In order to establish a personal relationship, I use the prospect's name often.
8. If I must leave the call for more than a minute, I offer to replace the call.
9. I return all calls promptly unless there is a good reason not to.

10. I treat all calls as important.

11. When I am listening, I make notes of what the prospect is saying.

12. I am courteous to whoever answers the phone.

13. Before leaving the phone, I make sure that prospects know that if anyone else contacts them before we speak again, to please let them know that I have been in touch with them and they are working directly with me.

14. I keep my calls brief and try to initiate the end of a conversation before the prospect does.

15. I am able to cut off a long-winded speaker nicely without being offensive.

16. I speak directly into the phone.

17. I am *"other oriented"* when on the phone. I try to be empathetic and understand the prospect's point of view.

18. I try to answer all questions patiently.

19. I am aware of the impact that nonverbal behavior has on the tone of a call and try to assume an appropriate physical and psychological posture.

20. I speak at a slightly slower pace than usual when I am talking on the phone.

21. I concentrate on using positive words and phrases on the phone and avoid negative ones.

22. I am a good listener when on the phone.

23. I try not to interrupt other parties when they are speaking to me.

24. During an important call, I let nothing distract me.

25. I am confident about speaking on the phone and approach telephone conversations with a positive mental attitude.

"Success is the sum of small efforts, repeated day in and day out."
-Robert Collier

Find Your Test Score

Give yourself 4 points for every *"Always"* answer; 2 points for every *"Sometimes,"* no points for *"Seldom."* Now add up your points.

92-100- Perfect score. Congratulations!

72-91-You have potential, but indicates you have much to learn.

0-71-You need help! Go to work on your communication and phone skills immediately.

Present To All Personalities

The highest paid distributors are paid in direct proportion to their ability to professionally present to all personalities.

❋ Make a favorable original contact.

❋ Skillfully and smoothly handle minor and major objections.

❋ We are first and foremost in the sales business. To understand and persuade others, we must study all personalities.

❋ People process information differently. Learn about all the different personalities and listen for what the prospects say, so that you can lead them in the direction they want to go with their own words.

"There is no one to stop you but yourself."
-R. David Thomas

Listen And Speak To Personality Voice Tones

Speak to prospects using their personality types in their tones with their words. Smart choice.

The Kinesthetic Prospect

The Kinesthetic prospect has very deep feelings. When they hurt, they hurt deeply, when happy they are the happiest people you will know, when frustrated, they withdraw or get distrustful. Here are some tips to listen for on your calls about the Kinesthetic. Listen to their words and then adapt your presentation to them.

* Are adaptable.
* Are easily disappointed.
* Are emotionally involved.
* Are into forgiveness.
* Are the heart-tug people.
* Are trustworthy.
* Consider the control type personality to be totally unfair, unkind, disruptive, and stressful to be around.
* Crave recognition.
* Crave security.
* Cry easily.
* Don't cross them, they don't forget.
* Don't like audio presentations.
* Don't like being talked at or talked over.
* Don't like being put on the spot.
* Don't preach at them or to them.
* Don't want facts and figures.
* Face to face is important.
* Fear rejection and when thinking of the possibility of being rejected, they become filled with fear.
* Fear abandonment.
* Fear disappointing others.
* Feel safe in numbers.
* Find it easy to share joy and grief.
* Get too involved with people.
* Have lots of feelings.
* Have positive body language.
* Integrity is paramount.
* Joy is greater to give.
* Learn to overcome objections and rejection and start radiating confidence.
* Like to be smiled at.
* Like to laugh.
* Loudest group of distributors.
* Love candles.
* Love family.
* Love props in meetings.
* Love to sing.
* Music moves their spirit.
* Need constant reassurance.
* Need eye contact.
* Need one to one.
* Need people to understand them.
* Need support.
* Need to be hugged and touched.
* Need to feel confident in what they are saying.
* Need to feel part of a team.
* Need to feel wanted, to belong, to be valued and if they do not feel this way, they don't stick around in Network Marketing for too long.
* Need to trust person presenting information.
* Need you to share ideas.
* Need empathy.
* Need to belong.
* Need to feel loved.
* Need you to be reliable.
* Need you to be sensitive to their needs.
* Need you to be sincere.
* Need you to take an interest in them.
* Need you to tell the truth, no white lies.
* See past appearances, can look at the inner person.
* Under extreme stress, they normally withdraw or get quiet.
* Want a people-to-people feeling.
* Want to be involved.
* Want to feel welcomed.
* Want to help a lot.

The Kinesthetic Distributor

Try to feel how others feel and consider where they are coming from before criticizing. Even if you can't feel the way they feel, at least try to put yourself in their place and have some sympathy. Don't stay in your own personality. Think of others. Don't be so sensitive. Remember, forget about yourself completely.

The Kino Voice

Most likely the Kino will have a soft, sweet, melodic, kind, timid, happy, hurt, enthusiastic, baby, or passionate voice. They want you to start the conversation in chitchat. They want to be included, invited, called to hear your voice, and feel needed. They are mainly belongers and don't want to be left out at any cost.

Their words: *"I feel," "I need," "I wish," "I care,"* or *"I hope."*

Distributors use these words: *"I was thinking of you." "You have been on my mind." "Want to go to a meeting with me tomorrow night?" "I've missed you." "I need you in my business." "I won't let you fail." "I believe in you."*

The Controlling Prospects

The extreme controller is overly aggressive and can come across as too dictatorial and can actually turn prospects away from listening to their presentation. They fear rejection, losing control, or being controlled ,and when sensing it happening, they get even more controlling. They believe their best defense is an overpowering involvement. Under stress, they normally get mad, upset and depressed. They vent their emotional anxiety by vocalizing hostility towards their upline or their company. They don't like to be interrupted. They want to feel heard and valued. They consider the empathetic type to be a true wimp. If you are too much of a control personality, you will not relate to the empathetic type personality. If you are this personality you want to work to develop more empathy and warmth. Then you will more easily help the empathetic type of buyer make the buying decision or the decision to join you.

The Controlling Distributor

Listen to the person you are talking with. Don't do all the talking. Stop every five sentences and ask a question. Be a better listener.

It's not about you feeling special! Make OTHERS feel special!

-Sarah Janell White

The Digital Prospect

The extreme Digital people are the numbers people, the scientists, detail oriented, no nonsense, accountants, who want the bottom line and seek understanding. Here are some tips to listen for about the Digitals. Listen to their words and then adapt your presentation to them.

* Are on time, and want you to be on time, too.
* Are not empathetic.
* Are organized.
* Are usually very opinionated.
* Can barely tolerate the kinos.
* Crave order.
* Crunch numbers.
* Demand punctuality.
* Don't like to be questioned.
* Have little time for chitchat.
* Have a know-it-all attitude.
* Have analysis-paralysis.
* Must do what you say you are going to do.
* Must understand the plan.
* Need details.
* Needs accuracy.
* Needs evidence of any claim.
* Need proof of income.
* Need systems.
* Need the bottom-line.
* Need to know Compensation Plan.
* Need to know how exponential growth occurs.
* Need to understand everything.
* Remember details.
* Talk numbers and stats.
* Talk bottom line, politics, history, speed of cars, make of cars, how much, how many, how long, how fast, how slow, temperatures.
* Use systems, files, and computers.
* Want data and sources.
* Want practical, specific details.
* Want to know exactly what it takes to join.
* Want to know exactly what to do to succeed.
* Want to know when they will make money.
* Want to know how they are paid.
* Want to know how much they will earn.
* Want percentages.
* Wants to be right.

The Digital Distributor

Have more patience with prospects. Listen for what they say. Don't start giving them stats when they could care less. Give more recognition to others. Don't assume they know that you appreciate them. Stop when you don't understand another's point of view. Seek first to understand and then to be understood. Don't be so demanding. Watch your voice, when upset, you can sound very mean, not knowing that you are very focused on what you have to say. This can be a big turn off to others.

The Digital Voice

Most likely will have a monotone, strong, stern, precise, clipped or in-charge voice. You don't want to just talk enthusiastically; they want to hear stats, facts and figures from you. They hate to waste time.

Their words: *"The bottom line,"* or *"Get to the point,"*
Distributors use these words: *"The bottom line is,"* *"My point is,"* or *"Does this make sense?"*

Don't be so stuck in your ways. Be willing to change and grow.

The Visual Prospect

The extreme Visual people look put together and want you to look neat and tidy at all times. They care about appearances and need you to paint the picture over the phone of how Network Marketing works. Show them the possibilities. Here are some tips to listen for on your calls about the Visuals. Listen to their words and then adapt your presentation to them.

* Are organized, and want you to be too.
* Are good at visualizing.
* Can envision the future.
* Cannot stand disorder, clutter, or disarray.
* Care about your appearance.
* Don't like messy handwriting.
* Like color.
* Like to watch videos.
* Like treasure maps.
* Like workbooks.
* Love pictures.
* Need ambiance.
* Need pictures.
* Need show and tell.
* Need the meeting room to be neat.
* Need to go to conferences, seminars, and conventions to learn.
* Need to see the Compensation Plan explained.
* Need to see what you are talking about on the call before joining you.
* Need you to explain with powerful words the big picture.
* Need you to paint the picture of their success.
* Need you to show that the business works.
* Need you to show them how to prospect.
* Say *"show me."*
* Want to see nice homes.
* Want to see the catalog and only want clean catalogs.
* Want to see you face to face.
* Want you to show them how to do the business.
* Want neatness.
* Want to see the circles drawn.
* Want to see copies of your checks.
* Want to see pride, and body language.
* Want to see you.
* Want upline to show they are successful.
* Want your car to be clean.
* Want your desk to be clean.
* Want your facial hair neat.
* Wear accessories.
* Wear clothes that match.

The Visual Distributor

Not everyone sees what you do. Paint the picture for your prospects. Let them see themselves succeeding. If they don't respond, it might be that you need to listen more. Look nice, clean your car, inside and out. Watch how you look. Trim all facial hair. Polish shoes, and wear no dirty shoes. Wash your hair, and keep a very clean look. Wear clothes that fit, not too tight, not too baggy.

The Visual Voice

Most likely you must use words to paint the picture of what they will be doing.

Their Words: *"I see." "I get the picture."*

Distributors use the words: *"Can you see yourself doing this?" "Can you visualize yourself jetting off to an exotic location?" "If I could show you a way..." "I can see that," "I see."*

Others might care less about the picture you paint. Present to all personalities.

The Auditory Prospect

The Auditory people have to hear from you about how the business is built. You cannot paint a picture for them, or send them packets of information. They need to hear about it verbally. Here are some tips to listen for on your calls about the Auditories. Listen to their words and then adapt your presentation to them.

* Ambience is unimportant.
* Are the best listeners.
* Are great trainers.
* Attend meetings.
* Capture information for their team.
* Debate.
* Distracted by noises, candy wrappers.
* Do great introducing speakers.
* Don't like you to draw pictures, just tell them.
* Have trouble following directions.
* Learn from hearing.
* Like being listened to.
* Like music.
* Like sizzle sessions.
* Like sound of their own voice.
* Love recognition.
* Love to talk, want to be connected.
* Need to hear information over and over.
* Need to hear reassuring words.
* Tell them like it is.
* Want to contribute to management.
* Want to hear clear information.
* Want to train.

The Auditory Distributor

Not everyone wants to hear you talk. Get some results and then be a trainer. Learn to be a better listener. Seek first to understand, don't gossip, and seek to get results. Don't hang on the phone. Talk with those who are going somewhere in business.

The Auditory Voice

Most likely the auditories will call you. They love to talk on the phone, they need to be connected, and they want to hear they are valuable, needed, liked, missed, and/or loved. They want to hear from you often by phone, want to share with you information and excitement. They want to discuss goals, the future, planning meetings, trip plans, compensation plans, want to tell you good and bad news, want to hear your voice, pass on gossip, call late at night, and need to feel connected.

Their words: *"I need to hear," "I hear what you are saying."*

Use the words: *"I want to tell you about my new business." "I want you to hear how you can get involved," "How does this sound so far?"*

Listen carefully to others. Don't talk so much.

Prepare For Differences

None of us is a single *"Personality Type"* but rather a composite of several types. There are signals that tip you off to easy ways to meet and successfully handle each one.

Here are some of the different types of people you will reach prospecting on the phone:

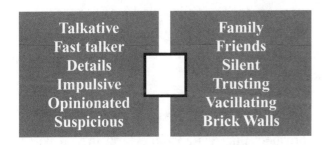

Talkative	Family
Fast talker	Friends
Details	Silent
Impulsive	Trusting
Opinionated	Vacillating
Suspicious	Brick Walls

The Talkative Prospect

Some prospects are by nature just plain talkative. The best technique is to give this type of prospect a reasonable length of time to *"talk themselves out."* They may finally say, *"Let's see now. You wanted to tell me about your opportunity?"* If, however, the prospect goes on and on about other talk besides the business at hand, the distributor must find some means of steering the conversation back to business. **Try this:** Pick up a comment the prospect has made and tie it in with the purpose of your call. **Example:** *"Your views about our economy are certainly interesting, Susie. The point you made about people spending more money at this time of the year ties right in with the opportunity I want to share with you."*

The Fast Talker Prospect

A fast-talking person likes action. They want to be told the highlights or essence of your opportunity, not the details; they want to be told fast, not in a slow or deliberate way. The rule is simple: pace your manner and delivery to match the prospect's tempo, not the other way around.

The Details Prospect

This prospect wants to have every question answered to their full satisfaction and likes to know every detail. There is no use in trying to hurry this prospect. You only succeed in irritating the prospect if the feeling is that you are trying to rush them into a decision. Be prepared to give details, statistics, and bottom line information.

The Impulsive Prospect

The impulsive prospect is apt to interrupt your presentation before you have had a chance to state your points. They might say, *"Okay, I am ready to join now"* or, *"No, I am not interested."* They also are likely to change their minds after announcing their decisions. It is often possible to get prospects to change their decision by quickly stating one more fact or benefit for consideration.

The Opinionated Prospect

The person with strong opinions must be *"guided"* into changing their mind. A skillful distributor can often lead the strong-minded prospect to listen and understand the benefits for them.

The Suspicious Prospect

The distrustful person suspects the world in general and is often convinced that every distributor met is trying to *"trick"* them into joining. They jump at every opportunity to turn everything you say or do into *"proof"* of why you shouldn't be trusted. The way to persuade this kind of prospect to buy is to *"soft-pedal"* yourself and your opportunity. Make no extravagant claims, *"tone down"* your presentation to avoid giving the prospect a chance to find fault with it. If you couple this procedure with an attitude that displays courtesy and deference, they will soon get the idea that you are not out to outsmart them, but that you are sincerely interested in serving them.

Friends and Family Prospects

When I first joined Network Marketing, I thought my friends and family would be as excited as I was. But that was not the way it unfolded. They were less than enthusiastic. I borrowed the money from my grandmother to buy the initial kit. I loved my products and just could not understand why my friends and family either were uninterested or would not help me succeed. It remains a mystery today. Instead of blaming them or being upset with them, I just let it go years ago and love them for being family and friends. If you don't expect excitement from your friends and family, you might save yourself some heartache. There are millions of people to prospect.

> *"Close scrutiny will show that most 'crisis situations' are…opportunities to either advance, or stay where you are."*
> -Maxwell Maltz

The Silent Treatment

The *"silent prospect"* is the most perplexing type for many distributors. You give your presentation, go into your closing remarks and the prospect remains silent, not indicating whether they are even thinking or listening. Ask questions that call for some response.
Example: *"Susie, I think this would benefit you, don't you agree?"* The value of this technique is that usually the response, even though it might be a monosyllable, will indicate fairly clearly how *the "silent prospect's"* mind is working. The *"one word"* tells you how well or how poorly you are faring, as accurately as does the more talkative person's longer response.

The Trusting Prospect

The prospect that has absolute faith in you will take everything you say as *"gospel"* and will almost always do what you recommend. Be careful to avoid misunderstandings and be sure that you tell the *"whole truth and nothing but the truth."* If the prospect finds, or even believes, that you have been misleading, they will very likely suspect everything you will ever tell them. When treated squarely, such prospects usually turn into *"solid"* distributors and are often your future leaders.

> *"Far better it is to dare mighty things, to win glorious triumphs, even though checkered by failure, than to rank with those poor spirits who neither enjoy much nor suffer much, because they live in the grey twilight that knows neither victory nor defeat."*
> -Theodore Roosevelt

Talking To Brick Walls

There are six barriers that can prevent your prospects from receiving and responding to your presentation. Prepare for calls by using the following techniques. These will help to eliminate or overcome communication barriers:

1. **Gender differences:** Thoughts and words that are totally insignificant to men can be significant giant thoughts to women. Things that women can see so vividly can be totally invisible to men.

2. **Personalities:** Personalities vary (see pages 69-70) Talk to the personality.

3. **Semantics:** If you use the exact word to ten different people, it can be interpreted ten different ways.

4. **Not agreeing with you:** As you begin your presentation, prospects may quickly have an opposing position or opinion that they have already formulated. They silently argue with what you are saying.

5. **Time:** Timing creates all sorts of challenges with calls. The prospect's mind is somewhere else the moment of your call. The prospect might not think this is the right time to be talking with you. They may feel anxious because you need more time than they want to give you.

6. **You:** There may be a number of things about you with which your prospect has a challenge. It might be your personality, your size, your image, your manner, your communication style, or the perceived validity of your expertise or opinions.

Help me understand what words you need to hear to join me?

The Vacillating Prospect

This prospect will usually accept help in arriving at a decision if assistance is properly offered. It is a mistake to move quickly with such a prospect. They respond best to guidance that is authoritative and deliberate. Points need to be repeated frequently and small facts explained. Do not give this prospect who vacillates a choice, but gradually focus the attention on a single course of action. When the information has been fully covered, and perhaps repeated, you want to bring the call to a close. This can be accomplished again by taking a firm position.

Example: *"Susie, we've gone over the whole opportunity thoroughly, and I am certain you will be pleased if you decide on joining. I know you don't want to rush into getting involved but really, I don't see how you could go wrong. The next step is for you to initial our form that I gave you (or will fax you, or I need your details) and you can get started immediately so you can begin to enjoy the benefits of being involved in this company."*

Think Through Cold Calling

Do doctors call you at random times to ask if you happen to be sick and in need of an appointment? Do dentists call you unexpectedly and ask if you have a toothache? Do mechanics call you without warning to find out if your car happens to be in need of repair? Of course not. ***But this is exactly what most prospects think when you cold call them.*** If you're lucky enough to find a prospect that is in a buying mode for your product, or wants to join you, chances are they will ask you to call them later.

Keep The Main Thing The Main Thing

Many *"overnight successes"* have spent years preparing themselves for the opportunity that finally affords them the lifestyle they deserve. When you specialize, you become better at what you do, you devote all your resources toward reaching your objective, you become more alert to opportunities, and you will reach decisions more quickly. Every call you make ultimately boils down to the question: *Will this help me reach my overall objective or won't it?* Having a definite purpose and a burning desire will help you focus all of your energies on making more calls. Your purpose will become your life; it will permeate your mind, both conscious and subconscious. You will make more calls.

Meet More People And Ask For Referrals

The more people you meet, and the more you pass out your printed material and get your name out, the more people you meet and can follow up and prospect. Talk to more people. Use STEAM. (page 67)

Exit Your House

Cold calling used to be *one* method of generating new business for many distributors. However, it has literally been ***decades*** since it has led in terms of massive results. Still, many distributors, continue to spend their productive time cold calling, instead of doing things that will bring them face-to-face with qualified prospects who want and need their products or services and are ready and even eager to buy. Hand out flyers, put out catalogs or capture names and phone numbers in lead boxes. See *Let's Party* book for many ideas. Available at www.janruhe.com.

One down and the BEST to go!

Consider The Source

Thousands of distributors have been mistrained and misled by otherwise well-meaning corporate trainers, distributors, and speakers. Distributors continue to bang their heads against the wall, wasting hour after hour and day after day cold calling with dismal to no results. However, the belief that *"cold calling works"* has been so frequently drilled into the minds of most distributors that they continue to do it, believing it will magically lead to success. Normally, it does not.

Get Out And Network

Some people find cold calls to be intrusive, annoying, disrespectful of their time and bothersome. Instead, Network. Get out and talk to people. Meet people and start conversations that lead to talking about what you do. Ask questions, be interested in others. Use STEAM, (see page 67) and follow up on those prospects you meet. The more your name gets out as someone determined, the more people will give you leads and referrals, and will take you seriously.

Seven Steps For Cold Calling

If you must cold call, here is a plan, but make this the last place to use your time.
1. Introduce yourself and ask if you may have time to explain your purpose.
2. Explain your purpose.
3. Describe how the other person will benefit from your product or opportunity.
4. Overcome objections and answer questions.
5. Ask for the business.
6. Ask for referrals.
7. End the call.

CHAPTER EIGHT
TAKE CHARGE

Take charge of the rest of your life. Network Marketing is a path in life that if you simply, powerfully, and with great confidence talk to enough people about your opportunity, you will succeed. You have to overcome rejection, pessimism, and critical people. Embrace the activities and skills that will cause you to really see how much more you are capable of doing, achieving and accomplishing. Shake up your beliefs, completely change your understanding of exactly who you are, what you can do and how much better, richer, more fulfilled and joyous your life can be. It's later than you think...

Struggle For Success

"The battle in life is, in most cases, fought uphill; and to win it without a struggle is perhaps to win it without honor. If there were no difficulties there would be no success; if there were nothing to struggle for, there would be nothing to be achieved."
-Samuel Smiles

Make Up Your Mind

"You make up your mind before you start. That sacrifice is part of the package."
-Rich DeVos

If You Don't Know Anyone

If you don't know anyone, join a club, get into a sports league, or volunteer. Every eagle knows a sparrow and every sparrow knows an eagle. Ask for referrals.

One Faithful Member

Ten team members were standing in a line, one disliked the leader and then there were nine. Nine ambitious members offered to work late, one forgot her promise and then there were only eight. Eight creative members had ideas good as Heaven, but one lost his enthusiasm, and then there were seven. Seven loyal members got into a fix, they got into a quarrel and then there were six. Six members remained, spirited and alive, one moved away and then there were just five. Five steadfast members wished there were more, one became indifferent and then there were four. Four chiseled members who never disagreed, 'til one complained of Mindy and then there were three. Three eager members - What do they do? One got discouraged and then there were only two. Two lonely members (our rhyme is nearly done) one joined the bridge club and then there was one. [Now for the value of one member!] One faithful member was feeling rather blue, but he remembered the neighbor, and then there were two. Two earnest members, each enrolled one more. Doubling that number and then there were four. Four determined members - They just couldn't wait 'Til each enrolled another and then there were eight. Eight excited members signed up sixteen more, and in another six verses there'll be a thousand twenty-four!

Are YOU the faithful member on your team?

The "T " Close

If prospects are undecided, help them to make a decision to join you. Ask prospects close to the end of the call to draw a letter "T" on a piece of paper. On one side of the "T" put a letter "P" for *"pros"* or WHY to join. On the other side of the "T" put the letter "C" for *"cons"* or why NOT join you.

Distributor: Ask the prospect: *"WHY would you like to join? What are you thinking? Let's put all the reasons or benefits for you joining right now under the "P" side of the "T."* Now help them think of 6-8 reasons why to join. See *Go Diamond* book for ideas. Available at www.janruhe.com. Next: Ask the prospect: *"Why wouldn't you join right now? Put your reasons under the "C" side of the "T".* Now, **SHUT UP**. Don't help them. Don't say a word. Stay totally quiet. Next say: *"Ok, now the idea is to see which side has more reasons for you to join or not join. Count up all your P's, or pro's or reasons to join now and how many do you have?"* LISTEN with interest and say *"Great! Now, how many "C's" do you have or cons or reasons not to join?"* LISTEN with interest and say: *"It seems the pro's win over the con's, welcome to (your company name) the next step is..."*

The Most Important Step

The most important step in making the call is to be prepared. The call has to be rehearsed in your mind without the prospect even answering the call.

> *"You have your whole life*
> *full of ordinary moments,*
> *why not create a few*
> *extra-ordinary moments?"*
> -Jodi Carville

Think Winter All Summer Long

The ants work all summer preparing for the winter. They don't start and stop. They get prepared ahead of time. Think about diving into getting ready for winter early in the spring. Make calls way ahead of summer to set up fairs, booths, convention plans, conference plans, seminar plans, and plan ahead.

Think Summer All Winter Long

Always be planning for the next event. Call everyone you know and tell them about upcoming events. Don't wait for your company or upline to plan an event, plan one yourself. You can have a coffee, a meeting at a MacDonald's, a meeting at a Church, or an Apartment complex, or at a Country Club, get creative. Build it and they will come. Dive into summer.

You've Got A Friend

"Winter, Spring, Summer or Fall,
all you gotta do is call and I'll be there,
yes I will, you've got a friend."
-Carol King

THE BOOKING LETTER

This letter is for those who do parties or personal shopping appointments. Create a letter that explains what you do, the dates you are available, and send out the letter as soon as you join your company. In the letter, explain that you will be calling in the next few days to schedule home parties. I scheduled 52 home parties a year for over six-seven years in a row using this **one** letter. You must make the calls to follow up.

Happy holidays! Thank you for an incredible year. I am a (your title) with (your company). Because of people like you, my group sales were over (put amount, for example $10,000) in product this year. I'm part of an organization that really cares about customer service. Satisfying your needs and wants is our top priority. So when you think of (your company name) think of me and not of running to a local store. I am only a phone call away. My phone number and website are (put them here). You are important and valuable to me. Serving you is my business. I love what I do. Being a sales rep for (company name) has been such a huge benefit to my family and me this year. It's been a perfect part-time job. I absolutely love what I do. This is my career. After the first of the year, I'll be calling you to see if you would like to schedule a party with me. Here's how that would benefit you (and list all the benefits). We will be partners for your party. You get the people there, and I will do the rest. If you would rather, just mail the enclosed form back to me, that will be fine too. If I don't hear right back from you, I'll just give you a quick call in the next two weeks to schedule your party. Here are my available dates for parties this year: Please circle your first and second choices. (List ALL of your available dates here.) As always, when you are one of my customers, you benefit even more, because you can always buy my product at 10% discount all year long. This is going to be a great year. I appreciate your business so much and look forward to being your (your company) sales rep. Thank you in advance. I'm looking forward to having a conversation with you in the next couple of weeks. Have your first and second choices marked and have your calendar ready. I'll be calling you soon.

Happy Holidays,
(Your name)

Follow up words: *"Did you get my letter?"*
"Can you schedule a party before the end of the month?"
or *"What day/month would you like your party?"*

CAUTION
"The Booking Letter"
could make you rich.

Ten Rules Of Prospecting Like A Pro

Prospecting can be much like working out. You know it is good for you and will produce excellent and predictable results, yet most distributors seem to avoid doing it. These rules make up a proven success formula for success.

1: Spend one hour each day prospecting. Prospecting requires discipline. Don't put it off until a later day when the circumstances will be better.

2: Make as many calls as possible. Take the time to properly define your target market. Make every call a quality call since you will only call those prospects who are most likely to buy your product or join your opportunity. Make as many calls as possible during the hour.

3: Make your calls brief. The objective of the prospecting call is to get an appointment or get prospects into your opportunity. The call should last approximately 3-5 minutes and should be focused on introducing yourself, your product, your opportunity, briefly understanding the prospect's needs, and getting the appointment.

4: Have a list of names and numbers before you call. If you are not prepared with a list of names, this will force you to devote much, if not all of your prospecting hour, to finding the names you need. Have at least a one-month supply of names prepared at all times.

5: Tolerate no interruptions.

6: Decide on times to make the calls. Traditional times to call are between 9am-5pm. Set aside one hour each day during this period to prospect. Some of your best calls will be done between 8-9am, between 12-1pm, and between 5-6:30pm.

7: Vary your call times. Many prospects are busy each Monday at 10am. If you cannot get through at this time, call this particular prospect at other times during the day or on other days.

8: Get organized. Consider using a computerized contact management system created on Excel. It can record a follow up call years in the future with no more difficulty than it would be to record one for tomorrow.

9: Get the appointment. In calling, the goal is to get the appointment or get people to join you on the phone or to book home parties and your plan, script, should be designed to achieve your goal.

10: Don't stop calling. Persistence is one of the key virtues in success. Most sales people quit after the first call. Most sales are made after the fifth call.

Expanding In Other Parts Of The Country/World

Ask everyone you know, who they know in the area you wish to expand to. Get the name and phone number of those prospects and call them and say: *"My company has given me the responsibility to find five key leaders in your area, would you be so kind as to listen to what I am looking for and give me some referrals."* Once you get the recruits happily involved in your opportunity, make sure you train them with your systems. Use the *Go Diamond Training System* to train long distance or locally. Available at www.janruhe.com. Either email it to new recruits or pop it in the mail and then call to go over it with them.

> *"The greater danger for most of us is not that our aim is too high and we miss it, but that it is too low and we reach it."*
> -Michelangelo

CHAPTER NINE
WATCH YOUR WORDS

Phone calls rely more on what words are said and the way they are said than do face to face conversations. More than 50% of the impression we make on others comes from nonverbal modes of communication such as facial expressions, eye contact, body posture and movement, dress, use of space and hand gestures. During phone presentations all of these nonverbal channels are missing. So during phone presentations, our voice, the words we choose and the way we say them are more important than they are in face-to-face meetings. The prospect has only your words and your manner of speaking to form an impression of you.

Decisions Are 95% Emotion

Give information on the calls by sharing your own words enthusiastically using words that can assist your prospect in perceiving the positive benefits. Pay attention to words that move people to listen, move their emotions, move their spirit, move their opinions, move their understanding and move them into action. Work on building your vocabulary so that your words paint the picture so that your prospect will get happily involved in your business.

"You will never know if you can achieve unless you try."
-John Hawkes

Jan Ruhe's Call Script

"Hi Debbie, this is Jan Ruhe. Susie Creamcheese has given me your name. I met her last night at the Bistro and she suggested that you might be very interested in doing what I am doing. Would this be a good time for me to tell you about it or would you prefer I call you back?" **If they say go on:** *"I am involved in a company called Happy Dance Company and we sell products online, from a catalog and in home parties that make you feel good, smell good, lose weight safely, make your children smart, cooking fun, and your home accents be beautiful. My company has given me the responsibility to find five new distributors in this area to represent these products part time or full time. You can make from a few hundred a month to thousands a month. How does this sound so far?"* Shut up and listen, then if no interest ask for referrals. If interested, say, *"the next step is..."*

It's What The Prospect Hears

You can say the exact words I do, or those who train you use and get either massive results or poor results. It's not just the words that are said, *but the way they are said that matters.*

The Three Rock Of Gibraltar Words

What Is Salz Streuen?

Do you know what this Dutch word means? The Dutch do, but others in the world do not although it's a common Dutch word. Here are some hints:

* They are good.
* They are hard.
* They are small.
* They are white.
* They come in a box or a sack.
* You can buy them at a store.
* Know what Salz Streuen are yet? This is what your prospects are doing. They are trying to understand what you are saying and are having a hard time getting what you are saying into their understanding. Here are some more clues:
* They are safe.
* They are not edible.
* They are used in many places in the world.
* They are good to use when it's cold outside.
* They are good to use on an icy sidewalk.
* Did you finally guess *Rock Salt?* You are right! Look how many clues you got before you **GUESSED**! The same happens in your phone calls. Prospects might not **GET** what you are saying until you have shared enough information that they can process it to understand it.

Two Small Words That Make A Gigantic Difference

Need Some Onions?

The person cooking a meal may say: *"I need an onion for this stew. John, run to the store quick and get me a pound of onions."* John may say: *"I'm not going all the way to the supermarket for that. I'm going to the corner deli."* The wage earner in the family may say *"NO way! We're not paying those big prices they charge at the deli."* Another member of the family may say *"But I love those big red onions they sell at the deli!"* A neighbor may pop up with *"I just saw those big red onions on sale at the vegetable store around the corner from the deli."* John may come back with, *"I've told you, I'm not going in there!"*

Don't Complicate It

Keep your recruiting uncomplicated by asking the prospect. *"Who besides yourself will be making the decision for you to join?"*

Hold Your Tongue

When you are upset, remember, that *anger* is only one letter short of *danger*. Great minds discuss ideas; average minds discuss event's and small minds discuss people. The tongue weighs practically nothing, but so few people can hold it.

"Good is the enemy of great."
-Jim Collins

Join Now! Join Now!

SWSWSW...next...SW

Some will want to join you or meet with you, some won't, so what? Who is next, someone is waiting!

Use Courtesy Words

The following simple but magic words and phrases create and maintain a positive image of the distributor: *"Please, thank you."*

Use The Prospect's Name

A fine way to let the prospect know they are important is to use their name on the phone several times. This is a compliment and personalizes the phone call.

People love to hear their name, so use their name frequently.

Call And Keep Calling

Don't get your feelings hurt. You will hear *"No thanks"* a lot. Start calling and keep making calls. If there is no interest, ask for referrals. If they hate you for calling, don't care, press on. Make that call.

WATCH MY SMOKE!

The Dream Stealers

As you set out to be a top distributor, there may be people who try to hold you back from succeeding. Some of them will want you to settle for living safely and doing what is expected of you, in other words, to conform. Most of those who seek to hold you back sincerely care about you, but simply do not understand your high goals. Don't let them steal your dream.

Protection From Rejection

Cancel out a negative thought and replace it with a positive thought. If you say something negative to yourself, stop and say: *"Cancel-Cancel"* or *"Better-Better."* Your mind will believe you. Do mental housekeeping often during the day. Give no one the permission to hurt or reject you.

Learn From Adversity

* Everyone faces disappointments. It may be a stepping-stone or a stumbling block, depending on the mental attitude with which it is faced.
* Failure and pain are one language through which nature speaks to every living creature.
* You are never a failure until you accept defeat as permanent and quit trying. It's always too soon to quit. Edison failed 10,000 times before perfecting the electric light bulb. Don't worry if you fail a few times. That's part of the business.

THERE ARE NO STATUES ERECTED TO REMEMBER THE CRITICS.

Prepare For Critics

Overcome the tug of people against you as you reach for high goals:

* Be single-minded.
* Drive only for one thing on which you have decided to achieve.
* If it looks as if you might be succeeding, all kinds of people, including some you thought were your loyal friends, will suddenly show up, to trip you, and break your spirit.
* Kind coaching and suggesting from those with a vested interest in you is not being critical.

Hint: If you are to become a top distributor, face the fact that the higher and more unusual your goals, the more others will try to discourage you from them, even in jest.

> *"It's a pretty good rule to remember that if the road is difficult, the end will be easy, whereas if the road is easy, the end may be difficult.*
> *If your pathway is filled with excellence, the future will be filled with comfort, peace of mind and satisfaction.*
> *Life was never intended to be merely a pleasure trip.*
> *It's a struggle, a testing and a training."*
> -Bob Holker

The Champion Creed

Learn this creed and teach it to your team.

> *I am not judged by the number of times I fail, but by the number of times I succeed. And the number of times I succeed is in direct proportion to the number of times I can fail and keep trying!*
> -Tom Hopkins

Conversation Principles

Use words that you are comfortable with that flow easily from you.

* Get to the point. Don't waste time with a long presentation filled with too many words.
* Be wary of babble.
* As you get to know the terminology (Comp Plan, Pay Plan, distributors, commission, Fee for service, recruiting, etc.) and you know and understand the jargon, the listener might not have a clue what you are talking about.
* Do not throw around curse words. They offend many people.

> *"Decide upon your major definite purpose in life and then organize all your activities around it."*
> -Brian Tracy

There's a lot of sale in a puppy dogs tail.

Learn To Love The "No's"

Your daily attitude towards life's no's will determine how far you will go. Use these self-instructions whenever you suffer any rejection. Know that you will hear **"NO"** many more times than you hear **"Yes."** You only need a few leaders to make Network Marketing work fantastically. **Learn these word for word:**

* I never see failure as failure, but only as a learning experience.
* I never see failure as failure, but only as the negative feedback I need to change course in my direction.
* I never see failure as failure, but only as the opportunity to develop my sense of humor.
* I never see failure as failure, but only as the opportunity to practice my techniques and perfect my performance.
* I never see failure as failure, but only as the game I must play to win.

-Tom Hopkins

Wording Your Guarantee

Everyone gives an unconditional guarantee. So what? Give an *"Increased Energy"* guarantee, a *"Greatest Taste in the World"* guarantee, a *"Feel Terrific"* guarantee, etc. Double the company's guarantee in dollars or add more time, whichever helps you and your product stand out and be more valuable. And don't worry. The small numbers of people who will take you up on the money-back guarantee always cost far less than the increase in profits you'll gain by offering it.

> *"The chains of habit are generally too small to be felt until they are too strong to be broken."*
> -Samuel Johnson

Forget the "Life Changing"

Share REASONABLE benefits. Forget touting *"life changing."* Be careful saying that because there is too much room for disappointment. Immediate results that are disappointing are bad for business.

Positive Self-Talk

Positive self-talk can have a powerful impact on sales and recruiting performance. Here are a few affirmations that you can use to build winning attitudes that lead to success. To make these affirmations work for you, tape this page on your mirror. Every morning select 2-3 affirmations, just as you would choose food from a menu and repeat them several times during the day.

Empower Yourself With Your Own Words

As you hear these affirmations, your mind will create new thought patterns and positive thoughts. These thoughts will generate new emotions and hope and confidence that will then generate more emotions, which in turn will trigger new actions that will lead to more successful results. Customize these affirmations so they closely match your ambitions, goals and values. Write your favorite affirmations on the back of your business card and repeat them before making your calls.

> *"Life is the path that you chose. Doors that have opened and closed. When will we forgive and forget? When will we live with conviction of the heart?"*
> -Kenny Loggins

Where Is The Conviction Of Your Heart?

When you sense that your chest tightens, or your stomachs starts churning, breathe through your nose and say to yourself with conviction:

* *"I always live in the delight and reality of being alive. My past is forever gone; my future is an uncertainty so I will be happy and thankful for each moment."*
* *"I strive to humble myself to others, controlling my ego and making other people feel important."*
* *"I am a professional challenge solver and I care more about my prospects than making the sale."*
* *"I am a winner, because of my contribution and cooperation we will keep on winning."*
* *"I am becoming the person I want to be and will end up doing a better job calling than ever before."*
* *"I am determined to work harder on myself than on my job."*
* *"I am first and foremost in the people business. I realize that they can only reject my presentation, not me."*
* *"I am learning every day."*
* *"I am proud to be a distributor in Network Marketing. Selling is the most important profession for creating new wealth. It is the foundation of the free enterprise system."*
* *"I can't win the game of Network Marketing unless I play. I refuse to take rejection personally and will make more calls and will work through these feelings of stress."*
* *"I continually invest time in study, learning how to better serve my fellow man."*
* *"I have clearly defined goals and I will pursue them today with enthusiasm, determination and discipline."*

* *"I keep on keeping on."*
* *"I know my growth in all areas is in direct proportion to the service I give to others."*
* *"I never take rejection personally."*
* *"I see every problem as an opportunity to overcome a challenge."*
* *"I will see failure as only a signpost on my road to success."*
* *"It does not matter what I want to sell, what matters is what my prospect wants to own."*
* *"Prosperity and abundance are coming my way."*
* *"The excellence of my service will determine the level of my income. Today, I'll give more than ever before."*
* *"Today I will do what I fear most and I will control my fear."*
* *"Today I will get myself out of the way and think more of my prospect's needs than of my success."*
* *"Today I will win. Why? I'll tell you why, because I have faith, courage and enthusiasm."*
* *"Today, I will not take advice from anyone who is more messed up that I am."*
* *"Today, I will see opportunity in every challenge offered to me by my company."*
* *"Today, I will talk to the right people at the right time for the betterment of all."*
* *"When I feel stress, I will consciously relax and let go of my stress before making the next call."*

THERE IS A DAY THAT YOU GET INTO NETWORK MARKETING, BUT NOTHING HAPPENS UNTIL THE DAY THAT NETWORK MARKETING GETS INTO YOU.

Use The Words "NEW" And "THE LATEST!"

Based on the proven fact that all of us crave the newest, the shiniest and the best, call past happy customers and inform them about the latest, new trip, new products, new catalog, new options, new anything.

Two Words Everyone Loves To Hear
YOU GET!

You Get, You Get, You Get

Everyone loves to hear the two words *You Get*. Say *"you get"* over and over in your calls. Share that getting involved will save money, bring more comfort, security, protect children, solve health challenges, make their home more livable, increase their income, add to their prestige, give them travel benefits, or other words that your product conveys.

The Word That Gets Attention More Than Any

Something For Everyone

Distributor: *"When you join our team, you will fit in great. There is something wonderful in our team for everyone."*

RED FLAG WORDS
When Talking To A Prospect

Say these words with **great emphasis**. If you have called someone or if a prospect has no interest:

"If your circumstances change in the future or if you change your mind and you think about joining us, please contact me. If in the meantime someone else contacts you about joining our opportunity, please tell them you are working with me and don't begin to work with them. It's important in our business that you contact me as I will be so eager to work with you."

People Buy Emotions

Keep in mind the prospect's feelings, hopes, desires, passions, visions, belief and wants, in choosing words you use.

> *I believe in you.*
>
> *You can depend on me.*
>
> *I won't let you fail.*

When In Doubt
Use Neutral Words

Sometimes, it's important to keep your comments neutral. If you use words with interest and voice inflection, you will keep the prospect talking. The reason to use these words is to encourage the prospect to keep speaking. It normally is clear over the phone when neutral comments are not made. The prospect might wonder if you are still there listening if you don't make some comment during their talking. Sometimes if you are eager to get a prospect to stop talking and if you only use these words you are conveying that you might not be that interested and the prospect will want to stop the progress of the call. Be careful using these words and only use a few at a time. Here are some neutral comments to make as the prospect is talking: *"All right, Carry on, Gee, Go on, Hmmmm, I see, Is that right, No kidding, Oh, that's interesting, Okay, Oo, Really, Sure, Tell me more, That is something to think about, Then what, Uh huh."*

> *"Keep my words positive... words become my behaviors. Keep my behaviors positive... behaviors become my habits. Keep my habits positive... habits become my values. Keep my values positive... values become my destiny."*
>
> -Gandhi

Use Short, Quickie Questions

Use quick, short questions at the end of a sentence that demand a *yes for an answer*. This must be used naturally and become part of your presentation. You can use a quickie question every five sentences. Listen to the response and carry on.

Example: Today, many people are looking for ways to earn extra money working from home, *wouldn't you agree?*

Couldn't it? Doesn't it? Don't you agree? Isn't it? Shouldn't it? Wasn't it? Wouldn't it?

**Do not interrupt.
Hear your prospect out.**

Ask a question every five sentences.

You Are Simply The Best

Use your words to convince the prospect that your company's products and opportunity and working with you are simply *the best* and are a bargain for the prospect.

Promise Exciting Benefits

Prospects are attracted to a plan, opportunity, words or products, which promise, for some reason, great profit or income, savings of time or effort, happiness or belonging. Make the idea of saving a sizeable sum of money especially appealing. Consider these openings on the call after you have introduced yourself:

* *Would a FREE trip for two to a fabulous destination interest you?*
* *Would an extra $300-$500 a month interest you?*
* *Would an opportunity to earn some holiday money interest you?*
* *Would you like to quit your job and stay at home with your children?*
* *Would you like to supplement your retirement income?*

Prospects having the need for one of these benefits will probably listen to you to see if what you are offering would work for them.

Warning: If you can't deliver the benefits in full, by all means avoid this approach. It will only be of use to you if the claim means exactly what it says.

Feel, Felt, Found

Use these words on your calls. Listen to what prospects say, then if appropriate say: *"I know how you feel, I have felt that way before myself and yet I found..."*

*"You're simply the best,
better than all the rest, better than anyone,
anyone I've ever met,
I hang on every word you say."*
-Tina Turner

*"Making calls can make you a fortune.
Be the one who makes the most
productive calls. Just do it!"*
-Carrie Leader

Setting Up Appointments

Here is a script to set up appointments from calls to use for prospects who call you responding to advertisements.

"Hello, may I speak with (first and last name)? Hi (first name). *This is* (your first and last name). *You called in regards to an advertisement about getting involved in* (your company). *Is this a good time?* (If no ask for when you can call them back, get a time.) If the answer is *"yes"* say: (prospect's name) *all I need is a few minutes of your time. I'll make this really quick. Can you spare a few minutes to hear that you can earn money at home?* (prospect's name) *as you heard in the voice mail when you responded to the ad, many people we are training are earning high figure incomes. Some earn from $200-$500 a month all the way up to 4-5-6 figures a month. I need to ask you a few questions and possibly set up an appointment with you or if you are ready to get involved, go on and get you into the opportunity now.* (If the lead is more than 24 hours old, then don't ask the first question, skip it and go on to the next question.)

1. *(Say the prospect's name) what did you like best about what you heard on the voice mail?*
2. *Great, tell me a little bit about yourself. Are you currently working and what is your occupation?*
3. *(Prospect's name) what type of income are you accustomed to?*
4. *(Prospect's name) What prompted you to call my ad?*
5. *(Prospect's name) it sounds like you have some talents and skills that would work well in what we do. I can't promise that it will be perfect for you until I meet you in person.* (Or go on and ask them if they would like to get involved right then over

the phone.) *So, here is what I suggest we do. I would like to set up an appointment to meet with you. How does your schedule look tomorrow afternoon? Great, do you have a pen? Please write down my name and number and if you are serious about meeting me, I would appreciate a phone call from you no later than 11am tomorrow morning to reconfirm. There is a restaurant near your house, let's meet there at 2pm. Looking forward to meeting you."*

IT'S CRITICAL:
Remember to ask for referrals if your prospect is NOT interested

These Words Mean The Opposite

My experience has shown me that if you have to say what you are, you probably aren't. *"I'm honest," "I'm ethical," "I'm in charge,"* are turn off words. Let your honesty and ethics shine through in who you are and how you act.

First Words On The Call
"Is this a good time to call?"

Work On Opening Words

Test the opening of your call for strength. You can't win attention and favorable action with an opening that is timid, difficult, complicated, negative, vague or irrelevant.

* **Timid:** A timid opening will never get the prospect to join you. (Timid) *"May I tell you a little bit about what I am doing?"* (Better words) *"I have found an opportunity that I think would be perfect for you. I must tell you about it today or tomorrow, when is a good time to talk or get together?"*

* **Difficult:** Anything that makes Network Marketing sound difficult should be avoided. Never say: *"It's difficult to get started."* (Substitute) *"Once you get this started it's like a train that has left the station."*

* **Complicated:** If you can't explain your plan on the back of a business card, it's too complicated.

* **Negative:** Anything that would create an unfavorable or unpleasant impression would be negative. Strive for a pleasant and positive reaction. (Negative) *"You probably wouldn't want to hear a presentation about a Home Based Business would you?"* (Positive) *"You must take a look at this opportunity, I thought of you and want to show you how you can get started right away!"*

* **Indirect or vague:** Opening words should not leave the listener in doubt. Be direct and specific. (Vague) *"Does the idea of making some extra money from home interest you?"* (More specific) *"Would an additional $300-$10,000+ a month interest you?"*

The Next Step Is...

Always be closing too soon and too often. Figure out your own pace of when to close. If you try to get someone to make a decision on the phone and they keep stalling, just ask, *"What else do you need to know to make a decision to join today?"* Use the words **"the next step is"** in every phone call that you make. Say… *"Well then, the next step is…."* *"I will call you tomorrow at 2pm"*, or *"Welcome to our team?"* or *"I need your credit card and expiry date and ship to address."*

Don't Use Rejection Words

Rejection words are any words or phrases that trigger fear and slow down the positive buying impulse.

1. Commission-Instead-***Fee for service***
2. Cost or price-Instead-***Investment***
3. Down payment-Instead-***Initial Investment***
4. Monthly payment-Instead-***Monthly Investment***
5. Contract-Instead-***Paperwork***
6. Buy-Instead-***Own***
7. Sell or sold-Instead-***Involve***
8. Sign-Instead-***Autograph, Endorse, Initial***
9. Deal-Instead-***Opportunity***
10. Pitch-Instead-***Presentation***
11. Problem-Instead-***Challenge***

How Are You Doing?

When prospects hear this they immediately think, *"What are you selling?"*

Take Care Or Take Charge?

Don't say: *"Take Care."* People who *"take care"* never get anywhere! *Take Charge!*

Words To Avoid

Abandoned, abuse, absurd, alibi, allege, beware, blame, can't, careless, cheap, commonplace, complain, condemn, coward, crazy, crooked, deadlock, decline, desert, die, disaster, discredit, dispute, don't, doubt, dummy, error, evict, failure, fault, fear, flagrant, flimsy, frankly, fraud, gloss over, guilty, hard, harp upon, hate, have to, hopeless, humiliate, ignorant, illiterate, implicate, impossible, insane, insolvent, in vain, jackass, jerk, jealousy, kill, lazy, liar, long winded, meager, misfortune negligence, need, obstacle, obstinate, opinionated, pain, poor, poverty, prejudiced, pretentious, quite frankly, retrench, rude, scared, shrink, sick, slack, squander, stagnant, standstill, stunted, stupid, superficial, tamper, tardy, timid, tired, try, unfair, unfortunate, unsuccessful, untimely, waste, weak, won't, worry, wrong, terrified.

Phrases To Avoid

* Interrupting, changing the subject prematurely, both should be avoided. Don't get careless with your answers.

* When you disrespect your prospect, you and you alone are defeating your progress.

* *"I thought I made that point clear,"* or *"You haven't understood what I've said"* - if you use these, you might as well hang up, you will have killed the call.

* Negative verbal reactions such as *"Yeah, right,"* or *"Give me a break,"* or the use of sarcasm are all disrespecting. Using declarative statements such as, *"You always do that,"* or *"You never do that,"* is disrespectful.

Dialing For Dollars

To get your business growing fast, double the amount of prospects you think you can call. Talk to everyone you can, on the phone and in person. Keep calling. You can be the best distributor in your town, but if you don't talk to enough prospects you will remain average. Call more people than you can meet face to face. Network Marketing is a numbers game. If you ever get discouraged, it's just that you aren't talking to enough people.

Are you putting prospects to sleep or firing them up with excitement?

Distributor Wants To Quit

If a distributor calls you to tell you they are leaving the business, say this: *"I trust your judgment to do that which is best for you and your family."* Don't let them slow you down.

There are reasons WHY distributors succeed and only excuses WHY they don't.

Reframe Your Words

Develop the habit of using words that are more positive during your calls. Read the following statements and see if you can tell which are more hopeful and positive.

"I can have the packet of information (or kit, etc.) to you this week."

"I won't be able to get that packet to you until later this week."

"I will have to check with my upline on your question and get back to you with an answer."

"I don't know anything about that."

"I am confident that you are going to do great!"

" You don't have to worry about failing."

"I have enough faith in you to know that you will follow through and get started right away."

"I don't want to hear any excuses."

"Here is what I can do."

"I can't do that."

"And the spelling of your name is?"

"Can you spell your name for me?"

"I am waiting for you to make a decision."

"Can't you make a decision?"

"The truth of the situation is…"

"I'm going to level with you."

Explaining The Bottom Line

Network Marketing is incredible, here is how it works: *"You will be sharing products and an opportunity for others to do the same. As you recruit people and teach them to sponsor people each one of these sponsored are joined to you in the Network Marketing System in your organization. You benefit from all of their efforts. The people you sponsor get customers to buy the products themselves and then they sponsor others to do the same in their circles of influence. As your team grows you have less and less direct input but your checks keep getter larger. If you don't object to or resist this opportunity, you will want to get involved and get started today."*

How Do I Make Money?

Duplicate what those who are at the top of our company today did and see what happens? Who knows? YOU might be one of those at the top in just a few months or years. So few people are willing to really work the business that if you do, you certainly can be among those at the top. Never ever give up. You can't be average and take this business or leave it, you have to go after it with a passion and an intense desire. Average is as close to the bottom as it is to the top. Our group produces champions.

What Do You Do?

Be known for what you do. Ask others what they do, take an interest, and they will ask you what you do.

Prospect: *"What do you do?"*

Distributor: *"I am a distributor for (company name). We have excellent products. We have a fantastic program that I would love to share with you. It took me awhile to understand what I was involved in but when I finally understood it, I became committed to this company and to my future success! And, we need people like you! Let's get together and let me tell you more and show you about it. You and your future matter to me."*

Getting the lifestyle is worth making the calls.

**Jan's footprints on Bengura Island
in Mozambique. No other people on the beach.
An amazing lifestyle awaits you, pack your bags.**

Is Network Marketing Easy?

Prospect: *"Is building a business in Network Marketing easy?"*

Distributor: *"Once distributors are successful and understand Network Marketing and it works for them, it seems easy. Just like anything else, you have to put in some time learning the business. Earn while you learn."*

Distributor: *"Of all the companies I have heard of, this one seems the easiest. We have products (that get results, gadgets not found anywhere else, products that people want, educates your children, calms your skin, helps you lose weight, jewelry and makeup that increases your beauty, kitchen tools to making cooking more enjoyable, increases the beauty of your home, makes cooking more enjoyable, or whatever benefits are derided from the products your company offers) and I am so excited about the products and opportunity that I just can't stay quiet about it!"*

Prospect: Let the prospect talk and when they give you an opening, say: *"You know, we were in the same situation." "I know of a distributor who was in that situation." "I was thinking about getting a job to help our family finances." "I was hesitant to…"* and off you go.

Speak with force and conviction. Remember to talk about **THEIR** interests rather than your own.

Make The Call

The phone is a huge part of our business. We can work our business anywhere with a phone and a calendar. We spend hours on the phone, prospecting, following up, scheduling home parties and appointments and talking and listening to people. We recruit prospects that we have never met, who had never seen the products that are eager to join by the words we use on the phone.

All Signs Point to

SUCCESS!

I've Stumbled Upon Approach

"I have stumbled upon the most fun job! I found out about a warehouse in California that is filled with educational toys that are not found in the stores. Someone asked me if I would like to be a distributor for this company and that if I shared the products with others and if they decided to do the same thing that I was doing, that the company would pay me a thank you bonus. I get a percentage on what I sell myself and then a bonus on top of that of what those I bring into the business get. You could do this too! You can do it part time or full time. How does this sound so far?"

THESE ARE THE BEST OF TIMES

Keep that rhino spirit and press on! Read *The Rhino Spirit*. Available at www.janruhe.com.

How To Use Words List

Try changing your vocabulary and use words that paint pictures or move emotions or get people to listen to your presentation. Those with better vocabularies sponsor more distributors. Use this fabulous word list to help you increase your phone skills. Keep this list near you when you are making the call. Choose 5-6 words a day and put them on a piece of paper or 3x5 card. Incorporate them into your call and watch your results. The better your vocabulary, the better your calls will be. Use powerful words on the phone.

Use Power Words

Achieve, Ability, Abundance, Accelerate, Accommodate, Accomplish, Action, Active, Adore, Advancement, Advantage, Adventure, Agree, Alive, Amazing, Amused, Animated, Anticipation, Appreciate, Approval, Attitude, Awesome, Beauty, Because, Belief, Believe, Benefit, Best, Better than, Big, Billionaire, Blessed, Bold, Boldness, Booming, Born to fly, Bouncy, Brave, Bright, Brilliant, Build,

Buoyant, Capable, Captivating, Carefree, Celebrate, Certainty, Champion, Change, Character, Charming, Cheer, Cheerful, Cheery, Cherish, Choice, Class, Clear, Climbing, Colossal, Commendable, Commitment, Compelled, Compete, Competitive, Concentrate, Confidence, Confident, Congratulations, Conscientious, Consistent, Constant, Consume, Convinced, Cooperation, Courtesy, Crave, Dare, Dazzle, Decent, Decide, Declare, Deep, Deliberate, Delighted, Dependable, Deserve, Despite, Determined, Destiny, Discover, Distinction, Don't be late, Dreams, Dreams come true, Driven, Dynamic, Eagle, Earn, Easy, Economical, Ecstatic, Effective, Efficient, Elated, Elegant, Empowered, Enchanted, Energetic, Energized, Energy, Enjoy, Enraptured, Enthralled, Enthusiastic, Epic, Excellent, Excited, Exciting, Exhilarant, Exhilarated, Expand, Expect, Expert, Explore, Explosive, Extraordinary, Exuberant, Exultant, Fabulous, Fair, Faith, Fancy-free, Fantastic, Fascinated, Festive, Finances, Fired up! Firm, Focused, Forceful, Forever, Fortune, Forward, Free, Freedom, Friend, Friendly, Fulfilling, Full, Fun, Future, Genuine, Giddy, Gifted, Give, Glad, Gleeful, Global, Glory, Goals, Gorgeous, Great, Grateful, Greatness, Guarantee, Guide, Handsome, Happy, Harmonious, Harvest, Health, Help, Helpful, Hero, High, High-spirited, Honesty, Hope, Horizon, Humble, Hyped, Ideal, Impassioned, Important, Improve, Improvement, Income, Incredible, Industrious, Influence, Initiative, Inspired, Integrity, Intelligence, Intend, Interested, Investment, Invincible, Jaunty, Jazzed, Jewels, Join me, Jolly, Jovial, Joy, Joyful, Joyous, Jubilant, Juiced, Kind, Knowledge, Lasting, Let's get this party started, Lifestyle, Light, Lighthearted, Live, Lively, Loyalty, Love, Magic, Magnetize, Majority, Make money, Massive, Master, Masterpiece, Mature, Maximum, Mega, Merit, Merry, Millionaire, Money, Monumental, Morale, Morals, Motivated, Music, Navigate, New, Notable, On fire with desire, Onward, Opportunities, Opportunity, Optimistic, Options, Opulence, Outrageous, Outstanding, Over the moon, Overjoyed, Passion, Passionate, Perfect, Perform, Performance, Perky, Permit, Personal growth and development, Phenomenal, Please, Pleasant, Pleased, Polished, Positive, Possibilities, Praise, Precocious, Prepare, Prestige, Priceless, Private, Produce, Productive, Productivity, Progress, Prosperity, Proud, Providence, Purpose, Rapturous, Reasonable, Recognition, Recommend, Regardless, Reliable, Rejoice, Reliable, Relish, Remarkable, Repent, Responsible, Results, Reward, Rhino, Rich, Rise, Safe, Satiated, Satisfy, Satisfied, Satisfying, Save, Search, Secure, Seize, Serene, Service, Share, Shine, Show, Significant, Simply the best, Sincere, Smashing, Smile, So fine, Soar, Sparkle, Specific, Spectacular, Spirit, Spirited, Stable, Stability, Strength, Strive, Strong, Study, Succeed, Success, Sunny, Superb, Superior, Supersedes, Supreme, Team, Teamwork, Terrific, Thank you, Thankful, The best, Thorough, Thoughtful, Thrilled, Thrive, Thrust, Tickled, Time to make choices, Together, Top, Tremendous, Trust, Truth, Ultimate, Unbelievable, Unbelievably, Unique, Unity, Unlimited, Unstoppable, Value, Valuable, Vibrant, Victorious, Victory, Vigorous, Vital, Vision, Visions, Vivacious, Wealth, Well done, Win, Winner, Winner, Within, Wisdom, Within, Wonderful, Worship, Worth, Worthy, You, Yours, Zestful, Zesty.

USE POWERFUL WORDS!

CHAPTER TEN
RECRUITING SCRIPTS

Here are my recruiting words to use in your recruiting presentation on the phone that will get your prospect to say *"Yes"* to your opportunity. Find ones that will work for you. Practice and learn several of these and make them a part of your presentation.

* *"Are you interested in products that make a difference and save you money?"*

* *"Hi, Susie, I'm checking out a new business called (your company name). I'm going to a presentation to check it out Friday night and wonder if you'd like to go with me and look at it too?"*

* *"Are there any questions you would like to ask me so I can answer all your questions?"*

* *"Are you ready to make your selection and begin enjoying the benefits of this great product?"*

* *"Are you working as well as parenting?"*

* *"Can you see yourself presenting these products?"*

* *"Congratulations, you've chosen to join a group of successful people who set goals and achieve them. We'll see to it that you do great."*

* *"Do you have 8 to 10 hours a week you could dedicate to building your MLM business?"*

* *"Have you heard of MLM or Network Marketing?"*

* *"Have you heard of my company?"*

* *"Do I have credibility with you? (Let them answer.) Then would you give me the courtesy of 10-15 minutes to listen about a company I am so excited about?"*

* *"I have found a way to pay our children's college tuition, retirement, pension and buy a new car. I'd love to set up a time to share this amazing opportunity with you, is Tuesday or Wednesday better for you?"*

* *"I help people start their own home-based businesses with no risk."*

* *"I just got involved with a company that sells fabulous natural, nontoxic, healthy products that we can buy wholesale and we can bring others into the business to do the same. We really need to talk about this. When can we get together?"*

* *"I've just found a company called (your company name). I think we can make some money if we work together on it. How does that sound?"*

* *"I've started a new business. I am a recruiter with a marketing company that markets (your product). It's fabulous. I'd love to tell you all about it some time... Why don't I call you and we'll get together. What's the best number to call you?"*

* *"If I could show you a way...to earn, to create, to make, to see, to have..."*

* *"If the right thing came along, and I mean it was really the right opportunity, would you have an interest in increasing your income and get more kicks out of life than you ever dreamed of? It's called (your company name) I'm not saying it would be for you, but take a look at it and see for yourself."*

* *"How does this sound?"*

* *"I am so anxious for you to begin to enjoy the benefits of these products."*

* *"If you had a job with no boss and no overhead*

expenses and could work your own hours at home with an outstanding income, would you be interested in hearing more?"

❋ "I am so looking forward to working with you! Let's get you going right now!"

❋ "I have my very own business, and I need help!"

❋ "I have so much fun working every day."

❋ "I love what I do. For (25) years I've represented an excellent company. If you want to travel, make new friends, make money and get more kicks out of life than you are presently getting, please tell me. How does this opportunity sound so far?"

❋ "I love what I do. I'm home every day when my children come home from school. I easily work around my family's schedule."

❋ "I want to answer all of your questions, so that you have nothing to think over."

❋ "I will help you. There are two trainings a month in our area, where you can attend over and over. This is a fun job to have!"

❋ "I'm anxious for others to meet you, you will add so much to the value of our team."

❋ "If I can tell you a way to help you get started successfully today, would you be ready to proceed with ordering your kit today?"

❋ "If I can tell you a way to make $200, $500, $1,000 or more a month would you like to hear about our company and product I just need 5-10 minutes of your time?"

❋ "If this makes sense to you, can we go ahead and fill in some paperwork that our company requires? You can go ahead and get your checkbook out and make out a check for only $25 to get you started."

❋ "If what I share with you in the next 5 to 10 minutes makes sense to you, could I assume we can move forward and get you happily buying these products, and share with you the benefits of being associated with what happens if you say "Yes," and what if you say "No" to joining me? Who else beside yourself will be involved?"

❋ "If you hear about four or more products you want, you need to become a distributor tonight."

❋ "Is there anyone else beside yourself who needs to make the final decision of getting involved with our company?"

❋ "It appears to me, after some of the information you've shared with me about yourself, that this might be a great part-time business for you."

❋ "It sounds like you really love parenting but need something of your own. Boy do I have the perfect opportunity for you."

❋ "Let's get you happily involved right now, so you can begin to enjoy the benefits of our products."

❋ "Our company has simple product and training manuals for you to refer to when you have questions."

❋ "Let's see if this makes sense to you, and if it does can I assume you'll be ready to make a commitment to join me today?"

❋ "Let's talk about the benefits of your being a member of my team."

❋ "My information coffee (or training) will be... and I want to introduce you as a new member of our dynamic team."

❋ "No one owns a customer. It's a courtesy to ask if the person to whom you are talking is currently working with someone else. If that person has not been contacted in a while, feel free to move ahead and work with him."

* "Now is the time to get involved with our company."

* "One of the great benefits of our company is that we don't encourage you to stockpile inventory."

* "One of the reasons our group is number one in the nation is that I ask you to pinpoint five people who will help you get started right away."

* "Our company's track record is quite impressive. We're growing fast (and cite the latest numbers if you know them). Now's the time to join."

* "Take the next 24 hours to make a few calls and set up 3-6 home parties. I know you can be successful but I want you to know you have business when your products arrive."

* "Our product is easy to demonstrate. If you believe in the product, you can sell it and recruit others to sell it."

* "Thank you for talking with me today. I'm hoping you're thinking about joining my company. I'm looking for people to represent our company part-time. If you are interested, please let me know now before I take up any more of your time."

* "That's why I sell (your product)! (You'd be surprised how often you can get this one in...)"

* "The income opportunity in MLM is unbeatable. Are you aware that you can rise in our compensation plan as fast as you want? Building a business does take time. You will receive big checks when you have a downline or successline of people each selling only a little bit."

* "The next step is to get out your checkbook or credit card and authorize the paperwork. Welcome to our company! "

* "We have monthly or weekly meetings in our area where you can come and get product knowledge, recognition and continued training on our compensation plan."

* "Welcome to my group. I'll be your coach."

* "What's your middle initial and to what address would you like your mail from our group and our company to be sent, so it can reach you right away? When you join us, your kit will arrive in just 6-8 days..."

* "You can get started today."

* "You know, the worst thing that can happen to you is that with a few parties you can have all these products, paid for a lifetime for your family."

* "You know, this isn't necessarily a lifetime commitment, and you need not make this the full-time career like I have. You owe it to yourself to try, though, you are too enthusiastic about this business to pass up the chance and I am too excited about you to let you go!"

* "Would you prefer to attend my November 1st or November 5th training?"

* "Thank you for the great service. May I ask you a question? Are you getting paid what you are worth here? I have a business I think you would love and achieve in. It's the best part-time business I have found. It will pay you what you are worth. Can we meet for a cup of coffee and I'll share it with you?"

* "We have found a terrific program for wellness and weight control that is getting excellent results. They are completely safe for your family

and saves you money every month, are you interested in hearing more?"

❋ *"You are right, can you believe how expensive everything is getting? We recently joined a great consumer discount company that is amazing. They offer savings on (your product) and you can actually build a business too."*

❋ *"I have three children and started looking for something to sell from home. I was invited to a home party, saw the products, fell in love with them and decided to give it a shot. Then I heard of distributors making an incredible amount of money a month and I decided to build the business. Now it is really growing. It's really simple compared to other jobs. No commuting, daycare, boss, or alarm clock. And I get to stay home. If you would like, I'll come over and share with you what I'm doing. Is tomorrow good for you?"*

❋ *"You must work a lot of hours, don't you? It seems you work hard for your money, don't you? I want to share with you about a business where my customers buy every week or month with no additional effort on my part. When can we set up a time to meet?"*

My Company Has Given Me...

"My Company has given me the responsibility to find five new distributors this week in your area to represent their products: Would you be interested in hearing more about it or if not, who do you know who might be, where do they live and how can I reach them?"

Share The Options

There are three starter kits.

Kit #1: *"If you have six or more hours a week to work the business, this is the kit to start with. This is the recommended option and you will start making money quickly. It includes (tell them what it includes)."*

Kit #2: *"If you have 4-6 hours a week to work the business, get this kit. It includes (tell them what it includes)."*

Kit #3: *"If you only have 3-4 hours a week, get this kit. This kit contains everything you need to get started. Give it a try."*

Do I Have To Recruit To Make Money?

Distributor: *"You make money on your own efforts, but if you want a larger income you will want to recruit and train others to do the same. Then you earn money on the efforts of others as well as yourself. While you can earn a substantial income by yourself, we encourage you to recruit and will teach you how to do it."*

Will You Teach Me How To Recruit?

Distributor: *"Our leaders have the reputation that they are the best trainers in our company. If you follow our systems and take action you will get all the support you can imagine. We won't let you fail. We have training in all kinds of forms, online, basic training, our upline's ezine, a loop just for distributors, teleconferencing classes, voice mail and so much more. All you have to do is to plug in to the systems, get excited and get started on your path to the top."*

CHAPTER ELEVEN
OBJECTIONS

Don't let objections slow you down. Learn from them. Collect them. Study how to overcome them. Sometimes, when a prospect says something to you that you think is negative or shows no interest, it is in fact a stall or a request for more information. Sometimes prospects fear having someone talk to them about something that includes selling or moving products. But as a top distributor you have to keep in mind that people are being *"Sold"* all the time in magazines, stores windows, online, holidays, sales and in every way companies can get attention. Objections are just part of what we must learn to overcome and handle.

How To Deal With Objections

Deal with objections by establishing the facts. Don't ever let your presentations get shot down by those negative know-it-alls or ill founded objections. Eliminate negative objections. Eliminate negative opinions and replace them with facts, facts that lead your prospect to make the success decision.

Tough times never last, but tough people do. The tough get tougher and won't be denied.

The Big Five Rules Of Handling Objections

Objections are not hard to overcome once you have mastered the basic rules you will be on your way to the top. You don't have to be put on the defensive by objections but will be in a strong offensive position when you know the words. These are the rules:

1. Don't fear objections. Have fun with them.
2. Deal with the objection as though it were a mere excuse or stall and go on with your presentation.
3. Capitalize the objection.
4. Find the hidden objection.
5. Obey the joining signal.

The Porcupine Approach

Think of every objection raised by a prospect as a question that you can answer and not as an objection. Get your prospect to think that they are raising a question and not posing an objection and you will put them in the frame of mind to listen for your answer. Answer a question with a question. If someone says, *"Does this product come in my kit?"* Reply: *"Would you like that product in your kit?"*

Prospect: *"The investment is too much!"* The real question is: *"Will I get my money's worth for the investment?"*

Distributor: *"What you are really asking me, aren't you, is whether you are going to get your money's worth?"*

Will the *REAL* objection please stand up?

The Personal "Answer Book"

Use a small notebook to keep a list of personal do's and don'ts and different objections you hear. After each call, ask yourself whether you've learned anything new for your *"Becoming a Better Networker"* list or your *"Answer Book."* Check with the notebook frequently to make sure your calls stay on the right track. What to do:

1. Get a binder or spiral notebook and list on a separate page each objection you are likely to meet in your call.

2. On each sheet, write the objection.

3. Write in answers to the objections.

4. Write in this: *"I am glad you brought that up, Mrs. Prospect. It gives me the opportunity to tell you some very important benefits to you to join."*

5. Study your *"Answer Book"*. It is your most valuable tool for increasing your earnings. Add more pages as you run into unexpected resistances that need solving just as you solved the expected objections. Don't hesitate to change a page when you have found through experience better ways to overcome objections.

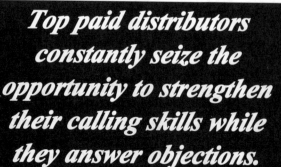

> *Top paid distributors constantly seize the opportunity to strengthen their calling skills while they answer objections.*

When To Go Into The Closing

When a joining signal is flashed you must:

* **Instantly stop your presentation, no matter if you are in the middle of a sentence, no matter if you have 1-10 more points to make.** No matter what you have planned to do, you must, when you are given a joining signal, stop making your presentation.

* **Express, in a matter of fact way, your reassurance that the prospect will not regret joining now**. *"I am sure you will never regret having joined today, I won't let you fail working with me."* Such reassurance, spoken slowly and calmly, is all that is needed. Go ahead and start getting all the information you need to get the prospect enrolled or with some other acknowledgement that the decision has been made that they are joining now.

Warning: If you don't stop talking on your call on a joining signal, you might lose the prospect. The prospect isn't asking you for more reasons to join; at this point they merely want your reassurance.

Restating Your Message

Instead of what you would do face to face, instead of an attentive posture, an interested facial expression and eye contact, restate ideas and make statements that indicate your attention and understanding.

Distributor: *"I understand your point of view and agree with you."* or *"I hear what you are saying and particularly support your last point."*

YOU CAN'T EMAIL YOUR EXCITEMENT, MAKE THAT CALL!

Capitalize On Objections

Every top distributor who is a big earner uses the technique of capitalizing on objections. If you have not yet developed that technique, begin immediately to master it.

Here is the formula: Answer the objection in such a way that you make your case even stronger than if the objection had not been raised.

Distributor: *"I am so glad you brought that up, as a matter of fact, this is how that part of the business actually works..."*

Is It Just An Excuse?

The proper initial response to any obstacle to selling is to deal with it as though it were a mere excuse or stall and go on with your presentation. You will quickly learn from applying this technique whether you are facing a true objection or one that is merely an excuse. If the objection is real, only that is substantial in the prospect's mind, you must meet it squarely. If the objection is a mere excuse, you will be able to by-pass it and get on with your presentation.

Suggestion: Do not ignore the excuse or stall when a prospect objects to giving you an appointment. Question their excuse or stall by saying: *"Tell me more about that..."*

Too Busy To Listen

You can make the *"busy"* prospect a listener. But before you can win them over, you must realize that the busy prospect comes in two *"sizes"*...either they are really too busy to listen, or they feel they must do something while the distributor gives the presentation.

Busy, Busy, Busy

Go along with the premise that the prospect is short of time. Ask for *"just 10-15 minutes"* of their time. And watch your time. By doing this you win attention because they will want to see if you live up to your word. **Note:** Isn't it interesting that the people who tell you they are so busy have the time to tell you that? Those who are truly busy accomplishing something, never talk about how busy they are.

"Yes, but..."

The alert distributor can easily swing the conversation from an excuse to some other point of discussion. The *"Yes, but."* Method is used perhaps more than any other.

Distributor: *"Yes, but when you consider that the benefits of extra money (or whatever their motive is) would benefit you starting now, it would seem to me that you have advantages in getting started now."*

Behold the word BUT ... what is true always comes right after the word BUT.

Create Your Dazzling Future!

Persist Without Pressure

It is wise to include in your words the assurance that you will only take a minimum of time and that the call will not obligate the prospect in any way. However, you can, and should, be persistent without being high-pressure. If real success is your goal, you can't afford to let negative reactions or objections side track you.

Prospect: *"Oh, I have already tried Network Marketing and it didn't work for me."* That should be your cue to try another approach like this:

Distributor: *"That's exactly why you would benefit from working with me, Susie. I have found a company that isn't about selling as much as I can, but to see that we move inventory out of the warehouse and into the hands of people who want and value our product. Why not let me show this opportunity to you. You might see a big difference and I won't let you fail working with me."*

No Need To Be Pushy

First begin to make your presentation. After the first 3-5 questions stop and ask a question, *"So, how does this sound so far?"*

> *This is not hard sell; it's heart sell. Good questions get to the heart of the challenge, objection or need very quickly without the prospect feeling like they are being pushed.*

Not Ready To Join

You will see that since nothing is lost by initially treating any obstacle as a mere excuse, or stall and that it is the proper one to begin with in most cases. If the obstacle is in fact an excuse, the tactic will dispose of it. If it is an objection, the prospect's reply to the attempt to by pass will bring out that it is not an excuse.

Prospect: *"I am just not ready to join yet."*

Distributor: *"Well, I know you are thinking it over, but I'd like to at least meet with you or keep in touch with you so that when it is the time you get involved in the business with me."* In this way the distributor doesn't get into being pushy.

In handling the objection in this way, you have avoided discussing the merit of the claim that it's not the right time to join. Now, if this objection is a mere excuse, it will be forgotten. As the prospect listens to you, meets with you or continues the conversation, if it all appeals to them, they will no doubt join in spite of the earlier statement to the contrary. But if this statement is a *true* objection, the prospect will not permit the distributor to dispose of it by ignoring it. They might tell you that you would both be wasting your time to look at getting involved at this time.

Uncertainty

Distributor: *"Do you understand what you need to do to get started and join me?"*

Prospect: *"Yes, sort of."*

Distributor: *"I noticed that you are not totally certain about that. What else do you want to know before you get started?"*

Listen And Press On

By passing the objection until the prospect has raised it for a second time saves you from making too much of it, and be too quick to pay attention to the objection. This is a fault of many experienced distributors but not the top producers, they just don't talk about it or tell you that they have figured this out. Ignoring the initial stall or excuse is sometimes useful toward the end of your presentation.

Example: Suppose that you are quite sure that your prospect is ready to join and then offers a lame excuse, one that you can recognize is merely a substitute for a pause before they autograph the paperwork. You might ignore the excuse, change the subject to something quite apart from joining and ask for the information to put on the joining form or the kit request form or any information your company needs to identify the new prospect as someone ready to join.

"I Can't Afford It"

You can't earn big commissions by trying to recruit prospects that really can't afford to get into your opportunity.

Prospect: *"I can't afford it."*

Distributor: *"Mrs. Prospect, I am glad you mentioned that, because one of the benefits to joining now is that it actually will save you money."*

BE CONSISTENTLY PERSISTENT!

Hidden Objection

If the prospect has an objection in their mind that has not been brought up, it acts as a barrier to the sale exactly as though it had been verbally expressed. And since such a mental reservation must be met, if it is to be overcome, the need arises to get it out in the open and discuss it. It becomes a part of good salesmanship, under such circumstances, to seek out the hidden objection.

Distributor: *"Susie, are you hesitating because you think you can't succeed at this?"*

Prospect: *"Well, yes! That's what bothers me actually!"*

Distributor: *"OK, now here is why I believe you can actually succeed at this..."*

Note: You must keep pressing for the unmentioned objection until you uncover it. Only then can you meet it squarely and get the prospect to join you.

Observation: Many prospects don't join because they are afraid to verbalize their fear of not succeeding.

Bad Publicity For Company

Prospect: *"I had a rep, didn't do what he/she said they were going to do, product always late, and I just don't think I want to do business with your company."*

Distributor: *"I am new in this area and the company myself, and I suppose I'll make some mistakes. But I know I won't build this area by not satisfying people. So the first thing I want to do is apologize for that distributor and hope you won't hold me responsible. I certainly intend to make my name known for excellence."*

Tried Before, It Didn't Work

Prospect: *"I have tried something like it a while ago and it didn't work. I am not interested."*

Distributor: *"Mr. Prospect, have you ever eaten a dinner that didn't agree with you? You didn't give up eating just because that dinner didn't work for you that one time, right? You say you've tried Network Marketing before but it didn't work. Is it possible that the plan itself is as good as you thought it was when you decided to try it years ago, but the only reason it didn't work was the training you had at the time. We have a system that's been tested over and over and it works!"*

Not The Right Time To Join

Prospect: *"I am in no hurry to join, if it's a good opportunity today, it will be good next month."*

Distributor: *"Really, it would be wise for you to get involved just as quickly as possible so you can begin to enjoy the benefits. Every day you put off joining, is just a day you miss out on building an amazing future. Let's get you involved today. What is your middle initial?"* (I got nine recruits in one day with this one script.)

Can't Get Off Work Can't Meet With You Too Far To Drive

Distributor: *"(Prospect's name) help me understand. We are talking about the possibility of earning a large income per month. You called in regards to my ad about this and it is important to your future to get involved right away. Why in the world did you call this ad if you weren't willing to get off work, drive an hour or two, or rearrange your schedule for an hour? Are you serious or not?"*

I Need To Know More

Prospect: *"I need to know a lot more before I join."*

Distributor: *"I would love to tell you more and that is why I would love to meet with you. I think once you meet with me and see what is possible, you will be so excited! You will want to get started right away."*

I Don't Know Anyone

Prospect: *"I don't know anyone."*

Distributor: *"That's why Network Marketing works so great. It's a wonderful way to get to know people. Thousands of people get involved in our company because it's so easy to just share this with your friends or family or even strangers."*

Normally the 6th objection is the real one!

Not Enough Time

Prospect: *"I simply don't have any time."*

Distributor: *"I know how you feel. When I got started I didn't think I was going to have enough time either. I was too busy making a living to make money, too, but I discovered with this program and all of the distributors working in this company that I didn't need much time to start earning serious money. I think you would agree it's worth giving up a few hours a week of your non-productive time to earn a six-figure income. Isn't it? Great, let me get some information from you so we can get you started making money."*

The Pessimist Partner/Spouse

The main way to gain support is by your own success. You cannot beg someone to be supportive. Sometimes, your excitement creates fear. Fear that if you are too successful, you might leave them. Fear because it's not a traditional way to do business. Fear because there is no check paid by an employer or benefit packages. Don't stay on the phone 24/7/365. It's so addicting to get a business going, but don't forget to spend quality time with those you love. Ask your spouse/partner to give you twelve months with **no** negativity to see what you can accomplish and that after that time period you will re-evaluate what you are doing. Share your goals with your spouse/partner. Tell them and show them what is possible.

Doesn't Have Any Money

Prospect: *"We can't afford to join at this time."*

Distributor: *"Actually, the money you will save is the most attractive feature of our opportunity. (Give stats, details and proof.) If it's the money that you base your decision on, I frankly don't see how you can afford to pass it up. Now is the time to take action so that in the future you don't have to say you can't afford anything. In fact, the fact that you can't afford it tells me this would perfect for you. Did you know that we have distributors in our Successline who have had garage sales to get the money for the kit or have borrowed it from their grandmother? Let's get you involved today. What is your middle initial?"*

If they have no money, tell them about me, that I borrowed money from my grandmother to buy the kit of products. If they don't have the funds to get started…move on, ask for referrals, or say:

"You're not alone. I talk to people every day who say they don't have money, but when they realize that for less than they will spend going to work for someone else this month they could start their own business and start on their own path to earn a six-figure income. They find a way to come up with a small amount of money to invest in a starter kit and off they go. Let me ask you this. If you had a horrible tooth ache, where would you get the money to go to the dentist? So if you really want to join, you can come up with the money. How bad do you want a change in your financial situation?"

IT'S CRITICAL: Remember to ask for referrals if your prospect is NOT interested

I Can't Sell To My Friends or Family

If you really believe that a friend or family member could benefit from using one or more of your products that might (improve their health, quality of life, have a prettier home, cook easier, smarter children, etc.) with the understanding that if no benefit is forthcoming, they could have their money back in full. Why would I not share this opportunity with others?

Already Contacted

Prospect: *"Someone else has called me about this."*
Distributor: *"Are you still working with that distributor? Has this contact been recent?"* (If it's been over three months since they have heard from that distributor, press on, who ever they are working with is not following up.) If it has been recent, then the BEST thing you can say is: *"That's great! Thank you for your time and I look forward to meeting you at a conference or upcoming meeting."*

IT'S NOT WHAT YOU KNOW, IT'S WHAT YOU SHOW.

Products Found Cheaper

Prospect: *"I can get your product just as easily from a store for less money."*
Distributor: *"Possibly, but there must be some reason, don't you think, why we do the largest volume in this part of the country? Most (or all) of our products are exclusive to our line. We have the best (toys, ingredients, gadgets, toothpaste, stamps, scrapbooks, kitchen tools, healing products, weight loss, or whatever your product is) on the planet. When you join you will wonder what you waited for? With the price of gasoline like it is, just think of the savings that you can make from just not driving to and from the store as well as the time saved parking and standing in line. Let's get you started today in the business, what is your middle initial?"*

Sorry, Not Interested At ALL

From time to time in making calls, you'll hear this mournful phrase before you ever get a chance to tell the prospect why you are calling. Prepare for it to happen. What do you do about this? After it has happened--and in the beginning of your career, especially, you can expect it to happen a few times and you can do nothing about it. It is unfortunate, but there are some people in the world who are just very poor-mannered. Don't argue; don't do anything that will reflect on your own good manners.

Before this happens, there's a lot you can do to prevent it. In some cases, you can write a note ahead that you will be calling. Most important of all is how you bounce back from disappointment.

How Many In The Area

Many people are worried that if they join you, that they will discover other distributors in the area. Don't tell a prospect on the phone (unless you absolutely know it's true) *"Oh, there is no one in your area building the business."* They join and find out there are several distributors in their area. Then distrust sets in. Always tell the truth. I WANTED to recruit my neighbors and people in my area so that no one else would. I attached fear that someone not on my team would come into my area so I had better recruit people in my area so they were in my Network. At one point, there were three distributors just on my street in Dallas, Texas.

Distributor: *"There could be others in your area in the business, but they are not terribly active, or they are building their business in another part of the city, or you won't just be building the business in your neighborhood, or there is plenty of business to go around."*

Rude Prospects

If the prospect does act rudely, before moving on to the next call, make a quick mental check to see why. Were you confident enough? Did you ask if it was a good time to call? Whatever you find, correct it before going on to the next call. If you do this conscientiously *"Sorry—not interested"* will be heard less and less and you will begin to hear, *"I'd love to hear more."*

**Don't let objections scare you.
They can be nothing more than a
way to ask for more information.**

Check With Partner/Spouse

During the first part of the presentation say, *"Who besides yourself will be making the decision to join?"* When you do, you won't hear this objection as much after that.

Prospect: *"I need to talk to my partner/spouse about this."*

Distributor: *"Susie, if it was just you and you didn't have to get approval from someone else, would you want to get involved?"* Point out that the partner/spouse might like the information directly from you. The partner/spouse can form that opinion by hearing about the benefits of the product from you too. Attempt to arrange an appointment at which both prospects will be present. Among spouses/partners, one often has a stronger influence than the other, either because of personality or partnership/marriage arrangements. At the joint meeting, try to detect which of the prospects will influence the decision and direct your strongest appeals to that prospect's values.

Distributor: *"Let me summarize the advantages of our opportunity so you will have the whole picture clearly in mind for your discussion. When will you be talking to your partner? I'd like to contact you as soon as possible to answer any other questions or concerns and get you started in the business right away."* (Then repeat main points.)

or say:

"Susie, I am a married woman myself and I know how it is. But once my husband saw a way he could retire early and play more golf, he got very excited about this opportunity."

No Jokes During Calls

Don't tell a joke on the phone unless it's clean and non-political or about religion or putting down anyone. EVER. Rise above those who waste time doing so.

I Am Discouraged

Distributor: If you are discouraged or thinking about quitting, say this to yourself…*I will succeed first, then I will quit.*

Never Ever Quit

*When things go wrong, as they sometimes will, when the road you're trudging seems all-uphill, when the funds are low, and the debts are high. And you want to smile, but you have to sigh, when care is pressing you down a bit. Rest if you must, but don't you quit! Life is queer with its twists and turns, as every one of us sometimes learns, and many a person turns about, when they might have won had they stuck it out. Don't give up though the pace seems slow-You may succeed with another blow! Often the struggler has given up when he might have captured the victor's cup; and he learned too late when the night came down, how close he was to the golden crown. Success is failure turned inside out—So stick to the fight when you are hardest hit, it's when things seem worst that **you must not quit.***

I Want To Think It Over

In this situation you have given your presentation and there is no decision. While they are *"thinking it over"* prior to your next meeting, you don't have to stop trying to convince them. Rather than doing nothing but wait for the reply, seize the opportunity they have given you by inaction. Often a first meeting may close on a rather vague note, with no firm appointment for a subsequent time to meet or talk on the phone. And that's the time to take the initiative.

Distributor: *"What is it that you need to think over, haven't I given you all the information you need to make a decision to get involved today?"*

Distributor: *"Great! Thinking it over means you are interested, correct, Susie?"*

Distributor: *"You are not saying that to get rid of me are you?"*

50% Of The Time *"Thinking It Over"* Normally Means Not *"Thinking It Over"*

What it *REALLY* means is: No money, can't decide on their own, no interest, doesn't like you, or your product, doesn't want to change, is lazy, or doesn't understand. The other 50% of the time they will join you.

Level with me, what do you need to *think over*?

The Ambassador Club

If someone you love or really like, says *no* to your opportunity, or customers who see your products and don't want them; and yet you don't want hurt feelings or guilt on anyone's part, suggest they take some of your catalogs, brochures, videos, CD's or DVD's and pass them out to people they might know who could possibly be interested. Tell them they can be a part of your Ambassador Club.

Make One More Call

When you think you are done with your calls, think about making *one more call*. When water is at 210 degrees Fahrenheit it is hot water, there is only one-degree difference between hot water and boiling water. When water is heated to 211 degrees Fahrenheit, it is simply boiling water. When the temperature reaches 212 degrees, only *one* degree higher, the water is converted into steam which is powerful enough to hurtle 60 tons of steel from a dead stop to 120 miles an hour in five seconds. It's the same in Network Marketing, those who do just a little bit more are those who get the bigger checks. Tell your story one more time.

> ## "Make calls today to change your life for the better forever."
> -Cathy Barber

Move (

If people don't like to talk with move on, they don't make Marketers. Network Marketi and you must call prospects and w... distributors and return phone calls and make calls! It's a huge part of what distributors do.

Let The Magic Begin

In the old days, many sales people made sales calls and got doors slammed in their faces. They had to do a lot of entertaining to get the sale. Today, still, in large corporations, the wining and dining continues…to get the sale. However, in Network Marketing, all we have to do is call all kinds of people and just ask them if they are interested in our products or opportunity and to help us spread the word. We only need a handful of distributors to make the Network Marketing magic begin.

"It's magic!"
- Bob Mega Webb

A Telling Statistic

* 44% of all distributors quit trying after the first call.
* 24% quit after making the second call.
* 14% quit after the third call.
* 12% quit after the fourth call.

This means 94% of all distributors quit after the fourth call. But 60% of all sales are made after the fourth call. So 94% of all distributors don't give themselves a chance at 60% of prospects. MAKE THAT CALL!

Get Results

Perhaps you have placed an ad in a newspaper to recruit distributors for your sales organization and you have received 100 calls. The point is not to merely receive lots of calls, but actually to recruit new distributors. Organize yourself and be prepared to make the most out of your phone calls.

Organize Information

Capture information for later use, whether it is calling lists, setting up conference calls, business opportunity meetings, or other follow-up.

Communicate Effectively

Have all information right in front of you. Have the correct information when you need it so that, when you are communicating by phone or in person, you have accurate product and opportunity information to perform your tasks effectively.

Practice, Practice, Practice

Role-play and practice to perfect your presentation so that they are effective and you aren't wasting time when you make them.

Don't Carry A Huge Day Planner

Have you seen people carrying giant planners? You don't want to look like Network Marketing is all time consuming. All you need is a calendar, a great attitude and your phone.

ASK, ASK, ASK

You may have the capacity, but you also have to have tenacity. To achieve, you must ask, ask, ask.

The Ring Binder System

Invest in a three-ring binder for logging outgoing and incoming calls. In your binder, keep notes on names, addresses, telephone numbers and other leads. Add scripts for dealing with *"various questions and objections."* Before you do your calls, have a special binder with scripts; questions and special needs that will help you make your interviews appear more professional when you are finally face to face. Remember, what is in it for them. Make the call about what is interesting to them. The more you talk, the more bored they will be. Ask a question every five sentences.

1. Obtain a three-ring binder, 1-2 inches in width, and a set of divider tab sheets from an office supply store. Expect to pay $10 or more depending on the binder you choose.

2. Identify and select the key areas of activities essential in operating your Network Marketing business like a career professional. Write these down on the tab part of the divider sheets and install them in an order that your business flows naturally as you conduct your business.

3. Develop an ability to target key information that is relevant to each section, and write that information on the divider tab sheets that separate each section from the other. Type or print them neatly, because if your clients and other distributors see these sheets you want them to be neat. You don't want to be embarrassed during your sponsoring and retail presentations.

GET ORGANIZED!

4. Use or access the information collected on the divider tab sheets and use this information as you work your business every day, in order to better perform the tasks required.

5. Develop the habit of logging and documenting each activity as it happens, i.e. logging the names, addresses and phone numbers of all the people you come in contact with regarding three-way calls, long distance sponsoring, referrals, retail sales, and successline interactions.

6. Make it a habit of using a daily, weekly or monthly calendar so you can schedule events, follow-up on future activities, and plan ahead.

7. Look at your calendar each day in an effort to responsibly fulfill the promises you made to clients, successline, prospects and other people. Focus on completing your calls, performing to-do tasks, and closing business arrangements ... not merely *"doing things"* or *"busy work"*.

8. Get every responsible person in your successline using a planning system as well. In this way, you will be able to know what they are doing, you will be able to assist them and you will role model that your business is serious and that your distributors should be serious about theirs as well.

"If you do more than you are paid to do, it is inevitable that you will eventually be paid for more than you do."

-W. Clement Stone

Tracking Logs

Three-Way Log- If you do three-way calls, make a section in your binder to remind you who and when you talked to three-way.

Three Months Out Log- Make a section of who you plan to call in three months or the new year, always keep adding to this list as you think of people who might be interested in joining or whose circumstances might change.

Ad Call Tracking Log- Placing ads can be expensive. To get a high return on your investment by improving the close ratio of your incoming ad, make a special section of your planner to track and follow up leads.

Compliment Log- After you ask if it is a good time to talk, the next step is to compliment the prospect.

Conference Call Log- Make good use of your time and your organization by getting distributors on conference calls. Can you make better use of your time giving a presentation to twenty people rather than twenty individual presentations? Conference calls are a key to training on a national and international level. Some top distributors send out email handouts and agendas prior to conference calls they make to their successlines. Starting words for a conference call could be: *"Hi everyone! Thank you for the outstanding job you are all doing. Let me call out some names of distributors who are who are going for greatness (then call out the names and if possible, results). Please push *6 to mute yourself or un-mute yourself during the question and answer part of the call. Does everyone have a pen and notepad to take notes?"*

Also, please focus on the call, it will be for 30 minutes or how long you want it to be.) Please make a note of the next conference call time and date (set the time and date and repeat this information at the end.) Tonight, I am going to cover just four topics, how to talk to more people, increasing prospecting, overcoming objections, and why now is the time to promote to the next level. " (make your own four topics)

Call Log- List on your Call Log the prospects that you must call quite often. These are prospects that are nearly ready to buy your products or join your business opportunity.

Golden Handcuff Log- Every December, start making calls to your top distributors and plan to have a meeting, retreat, holiday party, another call or some kind of communication about what will be happening in January. Bridge from one year to the next by making calls. Put your top prospects and top distributors on this log.

Interview Log- Keep a record of your interviewees and what you plan to say to them or when you plan to follow up with them.

Long Distance Log- Log all outbound mailings, such as letters, tapes, promotional materials, brochures, etc. In this section, you will note where your sales aid marketing materials are sent so you can follow up with phone calls.

> *"If you think you are too small to make a difference, try going to bed with a mosquito in the room."*
> -Anita Rodick

Opportunity Meeting Log- On this log, track information of those brought to business opportunity meetings or company demonstrations.

Prospect Call Log- Here is where 90% of your prospects will originally be entered. This is a place where you want to spend much time.

Referral Log- You will constantly be asking for referrals for both retail and business opportunity aspects of the business. List names, making special notes, discussing the status of the referrals and keeping track of the progress of the referrals.

Retail Log- Track your outgoing inventory of product that people call you for.

VIP Prospect Follow-Up Log- This is a section for prospects that require special attention and lots of notes, trade show connections, and corporate accounts. (VIP=Very Important Prospect)

Champion Log- In this section of your planner, keep track of who the strong distributors are and keep in touch with them. Organize contact information on your front-line distributors and those who are really working the business the most.

Long Distance Training Log- When calling your out-of-town group each week, training them on recruiting, promoting and selling keep track. This is the place to keep scheduled calls, of out-of-town momentum and progress.

BUILD LEADERS AND MAKE
THEM SUCCESSFUL!

Leaders by Location Log- This is a national/international business and you might be called upon to recommend responsible leaders in a geographic area.

News, Events and Awards Log- Network Marketers want their uplines to have current information about conventions, conferences, seminars, dates, upcoming meetings and recognition. Track in this section upcoming events, making sure that your successline are aware of current award and bonus competitions, upcoming rallies and major trips.

Ending The Call Scripts

Practice and learn ending words: *"The next step is…"* *"So, how does this sound, are you ready to join, schedule a party, place an order, etc?"* *"Now all you have to do is get your credit card out and let's order your kit!"* *"After hearing about the benefits, where do you see yourself fitting in to our organization? Are you going to go for it big time, or just see how it goes?"* or *"The next training call will be on November 13 at 2pm or the next Really Big Show will be on Thursday, March 7 at 12:25pm Eastern time. Be sure you are on it and listening in! All it takes is to hear one idea that can change your life for the better forever."*

> "Things may come to those who wait, but only the things left by those who hustle."
>
> -Abraham Lincoln

Q and A Cheat Sheet

Make time for question and answer time on your calls. Think ahead about what questions your prospects want to ask. Most likely they want to know what the total investment is, how can they get out easily if Network Marketing doesn't work for them, will you train them, how you train them, how fast can they make money, are there any territories, how many distributors are in the area, are there minimums, etc. *"Before I tell you more about this exciting opportunity, do you have any questions that you want me to answer first."*

Powerful Booking Blitzes

Decide on a date and get your team to have phone logs ready to go and on the selected date, have everyone call to book parties, get recruits, keep in touch, contact old customers, and generally stay on the phone all at the same time. Ask them all to let you know their results and post them on your website or email loop. This creates a lot of fun and excitement and activity.

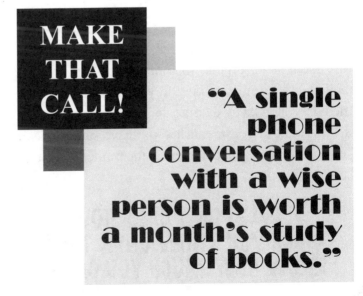

MAKE THAT CALL!

"A single phone conversation with a wise person is worth a month's study of books."

Challenges With Others

When you are having a challenge with anyone in your life, it's best to make a call and either mop it up, apologize, or at least open up communication.

Have You Upset Someone?

Have you upset someone in your life and messed up and want to fix it? Here is what to do:

✽ Call them and identify yourself.
✽ Acknowledge how the relationship ended.
✽ Acknowledge that you really do care about them and want to try to fix what went wrong.

Example:

"Hi, remember me? I know the last time we talked was not very pleasant and I regret it very much. I am just calling to tell you one thing. I have more positive memories of our relationship than I have negative. In spite of some challenges from my opinions and viewpoint, I am sure some from your opinions and viewpoint, I just want you to know that I really care about you and I want to resolve our differences."

Tell the listener that they don't have to say anything unless they wish to. Just let them know that you truly care about them and that you hope their life is great. If they are not open to talking to you, at least you have tried. Let them know that the door is open on your end if they want to consider what you have said and call you back or have you call them in the future. Make that call.

PEOPLE DON'T CARE HOW MUCH YOU KNOW UNTIL THEY KNOW HOW MUCH YOU CARE.

Rule of five: Every day make five calls that will move your business forward.

Have You Lost Touch With Someone?

Have you lost touch with someone you care about and you are hesitant calling this person? Here is what to do:

✽ Call them and identify yourself.
✽ Acknowledge how the relationship ended.
✽ Create a new connection with them.

Example:

"Hi, remember me? I sure remember you and I miss you. You know, I have been so selfish. I have been caught up in my own life and I know you are probably caught up in yours too. We haven't talked for so long, it feels strange to even call you. You may be busy right now and that's okay. I just wanted to call you for one minute to let you know that I am thinking of you and I car about you. Even though we don't talk all the time, you are on my mind many times?"

I JUST CALLED TO SAY I CARE

AGENDA FOR TEAM PHONE CALLS
FIRE UP!

MONTH:	FOCUS:
AGENDA	**SCRIPT**
GREETING:	
CALL TO ACTION:	

AGENDA FOR PHONE CALLS

NAME	TELEPHONE NUMBER	AGENDA/COMMENTS

THE EASY SYSTEM
TODAY'S PLAN and CALL RECORD
DATE _____

TODAY'S PLAN
This is my plan for the day (to be made out in advance of calls).
List calls in the order I plan to make them, including more than I expect to make.

NAME	PHONE NUMBER	OBJECTIVE	RESULTS

CALL RECORD
At the end of the day, record the results of your calls.
List classifications (N-R-C). Transfer pertinent data on each call to permanent prospects and customer records.

RESULTS SUMMARY	NO.	NEW RECRUITS/REFERRALS NAMES	ORDERS TAKEN					
			ORDER #		ORDER #		ORDER #	
				AMT		AMT		AMT
New Recruit (NR)								
Referral (R)								
Product Order (PO)								
Booked a Party (BP)								
Other (O)								
TOTAL								

A Message From the Author

When writing *Make That Call*, it was my intention to deliver my message in as short a space as possible and not try to explain all of the techniques I used in depth. One reason was that I have written extensively about Network Marketing in my previously published books. Here are those references:

1. The Master Presentation Guide: I discuss the preparation and delivery for a presentation. There are over 1,000 opening lines for your phone presentations.

2. MLM Nuts $ Bolts: When you get a recruit on the phone you will want to be able to train them on how to succeed in Network Marketing. This is one of the premier books on Network Marketing worldwide.

3. The Lady of the Rings: This is a book for new recruits to help them learn the ten most important concepts to master Network Marketing. An easy, quick, must read.

4. The Rhino Spirit: Having gone through some major upheavals in my life and business, I searched for quotes, poems and stories that would inspire me to continue to press onward in life. These are a collection of those stories that kept me going.

5. Fire Up!: This book will help you with your attitude and will help you keep a fired up spirit forever.

6. True Leadership: I co-authored this book with Art Burleigh, USA. We interviewed top leaders in Network Marketing and discovered their secrets. When you go into leadership, you will need this book to guide you along your path.

7. Go Diamond: I co-authored this book with Jayne Leach, UK. We updated my original Duplicatable Training System that will help you train others to go to the top of your Pay Plan.

8. Let's Party!: This is the definitive guide for Party Planning. My organization has held over one million home parties in my career. Everyone in Party Plan needs this book.

All of these books are available online at www.janruhe.com in the USA call 1-970-927-9380 or email BillRuhe@fireup.com

About the Author

Jan Ruhe with over 25 years of experience, has personally made over 100,000 phone calls in her career. She invested $250 into a kit of products in 1980 and turned that investment into a multi-million dollar business. She was a single mother for five years, in debt over six figures, raised three children and built a powerful Network Marketing business. She blazed the trail and has trained over 100,000 distributors worldwide on how to get to the top of Network Marketing. Want to know what worked for her? Devour *Make That Call!*

Here is to your success in making phone calls... "Make That Call!"

Jan Ruhe